794.8
NEW

DBS Library
13/14 Aungier Street
Dublin 2
Phone: 01-4177572

100 VIDEOGAMES

BFI SCREEN GUIDES

James Newman & Iain Simons

 Publishing

For Martha Newman

First published in 2007 by the
BRITISH FILM INSTITUTE
21 Stephen Street, London W1T 1LN

The British Film Institute's purpose is to champion moving image culture in all its
richness and diversity across the UK, for the benefit of as wide an audience as
possible, and to create and encourage debate.

Series cover design: Paul Wright
Cover image: *Pac-Man* (Midway, 1980)
Series design: Ketchup/couch
Set by Fakenham Photosetting Limited, Fakenham, Norfolk
Printed in the UK by The Cromwell Press, Trowbridge, Wiltshire

British Library Cataloguing-in-Publication Data
A catalogue record for this book is available from the British Library

ISBN 978–1–84457–162–8 (pbk)
ISBN 978–1–84457–161–1 (hbk)

Contents

Introduction

Lists are rubbish

No audience of contemporary media can have failed to notice the popularity and prevalence of the list. Post-2000 television schedules heave under considerable weight of the 50 Best or 25 Worst of almost anything one cares, or cares not, to imagine. From sitcoms to screen kisses, there is surely nothing that cannot be ordered, ranked and repackaged as a list for convenient, bite-sized consumption. Perhaps it is symptomatic of a society seemingly obsessed with league tables and a need to rate and attribute relative value to every product and service lest time or money be wasted on anything but the Best (or at least something from the Top 10). The trouble with lists, certainly the kind that has become a near-constant and largely unwelcome companion of the modern television viewer, is that they are usually cheap, lazy and, for the most part, as uninspiring as they are uninspired. They so rarely define their terms and render themselves practically meaningless. 'Best' according to what criteria? And perhaps more pointedly, according to whose criteria?

Like many people, our Top 50 Worst Media Products would include a fair number of list shows and books and so when we were approached by the BFI to produce a book entitled *100 Videogames* we were naturally a little reticent. The concern centred on the rubric for the list. In what way should one go about defining the 100 videogames? How could one ensure that the list was both complete and impartial?

The worst thing about 'best'

The most obvious starting point was critical acclaim. After all, videogames, like film, have been supported and sustained by a rich and vibrant magazine and journalistic culture that has offered extensive commentary and criticism since the late 1970s–early 1980s. Surveying and filtering through this mass of review literature one could surely uncover the most lauded titles of the last twenty-five years verified by a panel of thousands of experts. The list would write itself. 100 *Best-reviewed* Videogames.

But, what does critical acclaim really tell us? In the world of videogames, just as in any other area of creative endeavour, critics tend to operate in a somewhat rarefied atmosphere. The videogame critic's insight frequently comes with the benefit of a deep knowledge of and passion for videogames, and while such enthusiasm, experience and scholarship is often helpful and even infectious, there is perhaps a danger of myopia. In so much professional critical writing on videogames, there is an obsession with the details rather than the bigger picture, with the minute intricacies of level design, the placement of objects in a scene, or the differences between difficulty settings, rather than the contribution to the way videogames are seen by gamers and non-gamers alike as a popular cultural form through their advertising, marketing or the way they play upon their synergistic relationship with other media, or with the very idea of play and playfulness itself. As such, there remains the possibility that the impact of the specific game under scrutiny, in terms not only of its lasting effect on other games but also upon other areas of media production not to mention upon popular culture in general, may go unrecognised.

Moreover, critical acclaim, even distilled, filtered and triangulated, does not necessarily equate with popularity or commercial success – and nor should it. If critics and reviewers do not hold the key, then perhaps the playing and buying public can help decide the best videogames. And so, for a while, we considered 100 Best-selling Videogames. Unfortunately, this was a similarly short-lived plan as videogames sales figures are notoriously unreliable. Publishers keen to inflate the apparent sales of their products are rightly proud of their data detailing astronomical numbers of 'units shipped'. How many of these units are converted into retail sales, however, how many languish as unsold and unwanted inventory in distribution warehouses, and how many get driven into the middle of the desert and buried in a huge pit, is nigh-on impossible to disentangle with any degree of certainty. Of course, while official data may be massaged in a variety of creative and inflationary ways, even the most exaggerated figures take no account of the shadow economy of videogaming. Various attempts have been made to quantify the extent of software piracy to the games industry, but its true value and cost is ultimately unknown.[1] Illegal activities such as downloading ROMs and ISOs,[2] copying, pirating and even the perfectly legitimate swapping and sharing of games all muddy the waters yet further and while it is recognised that the true victims of online filesharing, CD and DVD duplication, and intellectual property theft are the owners of the content, writers of 100 *Best-selling* Videogames volumes are not unaffected.

Even if we could compensate for, or ideally eradicate, the illegal practices and accurately quantify sales figures for videogames, we would still be left asking ourselves what these really tell us. The shelves of any videogame fan will be well stocked with boxes usually covering a range of genres and platforms, perhaps building through time into a cherished collection. Each box brings with it the memory of queuing in a shop, clicking a 'Buy Now' button or tearing wrapping paper. Each game is paid for but is each game equal? Not equal in monetary value, necessarily, as titles have always attracted differential pricing depending on platform and proximity to release, but equal in *value*. On any gamer's shelf, some discs and cartridges will be dog-eared and battered betraying their near-constant use, some will be missing their packaging, lost somewhere in the mists of time en route to the house of a friend or colleague to share the fun, some will be played and replayed every month, week or even year. Yet some will be in almost pristine condition

– played once, perhaps not even to conclusion, and never returned to. What price these purchases? And how to quantify the 100 *Best-loved* Videogames?

Better than best

For all the initial problems encountered in attempting to establish a rubric for the list, it remained clear that such an undertaking is utterly essential and timely. Over the last forty years, videogames have emerged as the most exciting and yet confusing and diverse media form. Different platforms and technologies see games played at home, in arcades, or on the move. Different interfaces see players controlling with joypads, steering wheels, or even by moving their entire bodies in front of a motion-sensing camera. Different structures of game offer short bursts of instant gratification to fill the few minutes wait before a bus arrives, or more than a hundred hours of deep strategising, puzzling and execution. This difference and diversity is, without doubt, exciting, but what is a newcomer to make of the field? Where should one start in order to find out about this dynamic media form? Amazingly, despite the forty years of development, the simple and unavoidable fact is that there is no agreed canon of videogames. Certainly, there are vague and imprecise assertions about seminal games and superstar developers and designers whose every work is a gift to players, but this is a far cry from a list of games that encapsulates that which is interesting, innovative, challenging and rewarding about videogames, or that captures the form's relationship with and location within the wider environment of media texts and popular culture. It follows that there is a real need for a map of this inventive and yet confusing field. This is where *100 Videogames* finds its niche.

The key is to jettison the idea of a list of the 'best' videogames (however we might choose to define this). This list, then, is not concerned with the best, rather in strict alphabetical order with no hint of ranking or relative merit, what is presented here is an explanation and analysis of a hundred of the most influential, important and just plain interesting videogames that the first forty years of development has to offer. Necessarily, because it does not deal in verifiable absolutes such as published sales figures or review scores, the list is, of course, incomplete and partial. However, freed from the tyranny of presenting a definitive 'Best 100', we argue that partiality is far from a problem here and is, instead, an important feature of the volume. We are mindful of the fact that the selection of the games for the canon is contentious and that we will privilege certain aspects of games and gaming history that might seem more or less important to other commentators, critics and players. It is our sincerest hope that the list will cause as many arguments and start as much discussion as it resolves. At least part of our project here is to stimulate dialogue and improve the quality of discourse on videogames.

What this book is (and isn't)

In conclusion, it is useful to clarify just what this volume seeks to be and, perhaps as importantly, what it seeks to avoid.

100 Videogames is categorically not a list of the best videogames irrespective of how this might be measured.

Accordingly, it is not a Buyer's Guide with which to inform the reader prior to a trip to their local videogame retailer or before firing up their browser and activating a PayPal account. That said, we would suggest that all of the games listed here are worthy of play as they highlight something interesting and noteworthy about the form or advance(d) it in some way. Indeed, many of the titles we have chosen here have been selected precisely because they reveal something fascinating about the nature of videogames as a form whether structurally as in the case of *Super Mario Bros.*, aesthetically as in the case of *Killer 7*, or in terms of the relationship between interactivity and narrative as is the case with *Half-Life 2* and *Fahrenheit*.

Just as *Fahrenheit* begins to pose some important definitional questions as to what, precisely, this thing we call a videogame really is, other titles on our list are included precisely because they push at the boundaries of the form. As we have noted before (Newman and Simons,

2004), the videogame form is characterised more by the extraordinary differences between individual titles than their similarities. Whether we consider the range of technologies that we make use of to play, the places we play, or the amounts of time we play for in a single sitting, the distinctions between mobile phone *Snake*, *EyeToy: Play*, or *Final Fantasy VII* surely far outnumber any possible commonalities. Add to this that a player soon learns that some games have clear outcomes and definite endings while others have no conclusion, some are random and are never the same twice, and some simply do not encourage the player to even think about things as linear as 'endings' or 'beginnings'. Games such as *Animal Crossing* or *The Sims* have no climactic denouement, per se, and may continue ad infinitum, plodding along at their own tempo unless of course the player sets themselves specific goals that are superimposed over the game's structure.

What is particularly interesting about the list of boundary-pushing titles is how many of them derive from the 'mainstream'. While titles such as *J. D. Spy* that brim with innovation and an inventiveness that is sometimes cruelly demanding for the player come from the independent development community, many of the titles we have singled out for interrogation here come from the world's biggest developers and publishers. *Nintendogs*, *Electroplankton*, *Trauma Center*, *Animal Crossing* are all among Nintendo's finest creations, while the EyeToy camera peripheral that allows the player to use their entire body to control the action on screen comes to us from Sony – not only a major player in videogames, but one of the biggest corporations in the world. Innovative, inventive and unexpected these developments may be yet their diversity does not help us in any way to reach a reliable and inclusive definition of videogames as a form, let alone fit into any genre type.

Fortunately, this book is not tasked with establishing such a definition and so complicating the issue for others whose job it will be later is a viable part of our mission. As such, the hundred videogames here should be seen as part of the canon of videogames' first forty years.

Whether any particular individual finds them enjoyable, pleasurable, fun, or wishes to own them or the platform upon which they are to be played, is not a consideration here.

Ultimately, *100 Videogames* serves a number of purposes and, accordingly, offers something of value to a number of different readers.

- The list is intended to be a means of interrogating, challenging and hopefully codifying the videogames industry's vague and unformed assumptions, and truisms regarding its own most important and seminal titles.
- It is a way of introducing the huge and diverse field of videogames for non-experts or those simply curious about this most important and pervasive of new media.
- Finally, it is something to argue with. It is not, and cannot be, a definitive list as not only will opinion differ, but the ground will continue to shift. The release of Nintendo's next-generation console, the Wii, complete with motion-sensing TV-remote-styled controller, may well mark a sea-change in the way videogames are played in the same way that EyeToy and Nintendo DS have before it. Certainly, Sony appear to have liked what they saw Nintendo doing with the pre-release Wii and have announced a similar though not identical functionality for the PlayStation 3 joypad.

The future of videogames looks set to be characterised by the same unpredictable and imaginative innovation and change that has defined the first forty years of the form. We can all look forward to a constantly evolving industry and form that makes 100 *More* Videogames a mouthwatering prospect . . .

James Newman and Iain Simons
June 2006

Notes

1. See <www.theesa.com/ip/anti_piracy_faq.php> and <www.elspa.com/?t=antipiracyunit> for more on US and European entertainment software piracy and initiatives.

2. ROMs (Read Only Memory) and ISOs (International Standards Organisation) are shorthand descriptors used in the gaming community to describe copies (usually known as 'dumps' or 'rips') of game cartridges, CD-ROMs, DVDs or even chips on Coin-Operated printed circuit boards much like mp3 rips of audio CDs. These dumps contain the game code, the computer program that instructs the hardware how to deal with graphics, sound, player input, as well as setting out the rules of the game. They can either be used in conjunction with the original hardware (though this often needs modification in order to run copied games), or under emulation. An emulator is a piece of software that allows one hardware platform to mimic the performance and functionality of another. Thus, it is possible to make a PC, Macintosh, PlayStation Portable, for example, behave like a Coin-Op cabinet, a Super Nintendo Entertainment System, or MegaDrive and run software in ROM or ISO format. The legality of playing videogames under emulation is much debated among the fan community though there is little doubt that duplicating software without permission constitutes copyright infringement.

1942
1984
Capcom

Originally released in 1984, this vertically scrolling shoot-em-up has been released on virtually every platform of significance since. The first game in what was to quickly become a franchise, it has lodged a firm place in the affections of gamers. The action sees the player flying through thirty-two levels of progressively more challenging aerial combat, taking on wave after wave (after wave) of enemy single-handedly.

Set during the Pacific air wars of World War II, the game attracted most criticism for its somewhat inaccurate depiction of warfare during that period. While it is probable that Capcom weren't aiming for either an historically, or technically accurate simulation of air combat – it still attracted fierce criticism from some quarters. *1942* alludes to a specific campaign and period in time and makes no attempt to veil any of the factions involved. This combat did not involve the destruction of anonymous aliens, or even anonymous troops – but specifically Japanese soldiers from a specific and identifiable campaign. As one Internet-based reviewer put it, '*1942* is unrealistic to an absurd degree . . . It's not a terrible cliché – you don't save any princesses – but I take offence when a bastardization of war (a human tragedy of the first degree) occurs.'[3] Quite what gravitas using such genuine source material offered the game is unclear, although the series continued to use the same war as contextual backdrop for another two sequels. The series only broke with this standard in the final title, *19XX*, which transferred the main gameplay to a fictional war which builds towards a nuclear apocalypse. It remains, of course, your single-handed responsibility to stop it.

Developer Yoshiki Okamoto, who had previously created *Time Pilot*, would go on to create a string of further seminal titles – perhaps most notably the *Street Fighter* series.

3. <www.gamefaqs.com/console/nes/review/R28493.html>.

Publisher: Capcom; **Platform**: Coin-Op.

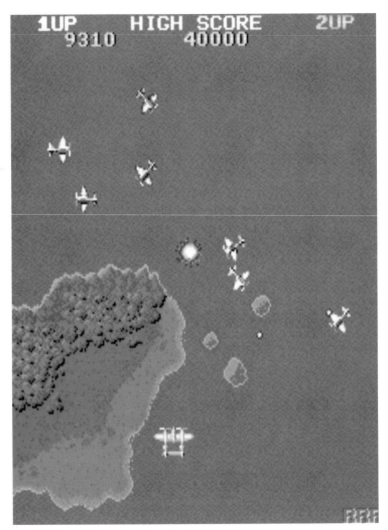

1942: 'unrealistic to an absurd degree' according to some

Advance Wars
2001
Intelligent Systems

The origins of the cultish *Advance Wars* titles actually date back to the *Famicom* and the first in the series *Famicom Wars*. Establishing the same style of turn-based strategy, which characterises the series they reached global popularity in 2001 when *Advance Wars* was released for the western market on the phenomenally successful GameBoy Advance.

A military strategy game, *Advance Wars* casts the player as the tactical advisor for the 'Orange Star' at the outset of the game. Equipped with a number of Commanding Officers (COs) all with differing strengths and weaknesses, the strategy lies in the use of the complex set of assets at your disposal to defeat the enemy forces. The crisp visual design of the game deserves special mention as it accurately – and entertainingly – describes an increasingly complex battlefield scenario on the limited display of the GameBoy Advance.

Advance Wars: rockets in your pocket

The game makes particular investment in the fusion of the contextual narrative with the core gameplay. Much exposition takes place before battles occur, delivered by the tested (and effective) device of character faces flying in and captions being spat across the screen. The capacity of this formula to actually generate drama is surprisingly effective (see also: *Trauma Center: Under the Knife*) and genuinely contributes to the campaign saga one is engaged in. Without this drama, *Advance Wars* would be a series of strategic encounters; with such factions characterised more fully the player finds himself engaged in the ongoing struggle, rather than simply the micro-battle. The game cleverly hints at the cultural markers of existing countries to reinforce these cues. American, British and Japanese forces of a time circa World War II are all recognisable. In particular, the faction ultimately revealed as being 'evil', entitled Black Hole, makes several subtle nods towards being Germanic Nazis. In a political statement possibly incompatible with 'Nintendo-ness', it was made clear in *Advance Wars 2* that the Black Hole force were actually aliens. *Advance Wars* continues to be a strong franchise on Nintendo platforms, with *Advance Wars Dual Strike* for the DS receiving critical acclaim in 2005.

The developer, Intelligent Systems, is worthy of particular attention having produced and contributed to some of the best-loved titles in the Nintendo family, including *Metroid*, *Paper Mario* and *WarioWare*.

Publisher: Nintendo; **Platform**: Nintendo GameBoy Advance.

Animal Crossing
2004 (Europe. Note: *Animal Forest* released in Japan 2001)
Nintendo Entertainment and Analysis Development

Nintendo calls it a communication game, but *Animal Crossing* is essentially interactive *Seinfeld*. Just like the classic US sitcom, *Animal Crossing* is funny, it is full of characters that are as loveable as they are irritating, and its moirés work their way into your life, speech and thoughts without you ever really noticing. But, notwithstanding these superficial similarities, there is a far more foundational connection between the game and television series. Famously, *Seinfeld* is 'a show about nothing', a show that focuses on the often excruciating minutiae and trivialities of everyday life; a show whose plotlines centre on activities as ordinary as the very act of watching television itself. *Animal Crossing* takes this basic premise and applies it to the videogame form. Indeed, it applies it in a more committed manner than *Seinfeld* and, in doing so, creates something utterly original, wholly revolutionary and shockingly compelling, from . . . nothing.

If a television show about nothing sounds curious, remember at least that the audience watches these acts of ordinariness play out in front of them, just as they did when Samuel Beckett crafted tableaux of inaction on the stage or Osborne made ironing the centrepiece of *Look Back in Anger*. However, a videogame is about participation and doing. Having one's attention drawn to the agony of routine and mundanity is one thing, but being asked to perform the chores and the waiting oneself should be quite another. And yet, *Animal Crossing* is among the most compelling and absorbing games, though compulsion here does not manifest itself in terms of mammoth single play-sessions. This is not a game that erodes evenings or where the sun rises before you have had a chance to go to bed after playing all night. Rather, this is a game that demands to be played frequently; ideally every day, and perhaps several times a day. This is a game that demands and rewards commitment.

All this from a game that does nothing more than simulate a small village, populated by a few animals, who talk and occasionally send one another letters. The world of *Animal Crossing* is one where the most exciting activities are digging for fossils, hunting insects and bugs, fishing, arranging furniture in your house to maximise feng shui or, better still, waiting with Godot-like anticipation to see what new items might be available in the village shop. One would be forgiven for thinking this sounds less than compelling. Certainly, there is pleasure in collecting and completism – any *Pokémon* player will recognise the lure of catching every species of fish while communication does indeed play a central role in the game. But *Animal Crossing* addiction does not come from the excitement of any one activity. Rather, the desire to return and replay comes because *Animal Crossing*'s is a persistent world that changes, develops and evolves whether you are visiting or not. Ultimately, it is the thought that something *might* happen while you are not there that keeps you coming back and spending so much time doing . . . nothing.

Talking to the animals in the village is the mainstay of the gameplay and their replies and ramblings are so charmingly witty, whimsical and offbeat, thanks to the semi-random way they are generated by the game engine, that they soon become real and rounded characters with clearly definable and differentiated personalities. Indeed, such is the fondness for these new friends, even the grumpy ones, that the news that an animal has decided to pack up their bags and leave the village for pastures new elicits feelings of genuine upset that even videogame aficionados will have rarely felt.

Given its unusual nature, it is perhaps unsurprising to learn that *Animal Crossing*'s path to release was somewhat complicated. Originally launched in 2001 as *Animal Forest* and available only in Japan for the Nintendo 64 console, the game was subsequently converted and updated for the GameCube. The game was retitled *Animal Crossing* for its 2002 US launch, while a much-delayed European release only materialised in 2004 after a protracted fan-led campaign and a necessarily lengthy localisation procedure to translate the animalese into seven European languages. The sequel, *Animal Crossing: Wild World,* for the Nintendo DS takes the game online and allows players throughout the world to visit one another's villages. While Japan and the US got to work in 2005, European players would have to wait until March 2006. Still, this is something – or rather nothing – worth waiting for.

Publisher: Nintendo; **Platform**: Nintendo GameCube.

Asteroids
1979
Atari

Asteroids belongs to the classic school of game design. It is simple almost to the point of being insulting. The player pilots a spacecraft that is equipped with a rocket booster to move and a laser with which to shoot and destroy everything on screen. The object of the game is equally uncomplicated. As everything in the nether world is hostile and intent on destroying the player's craft either by wit or accident, it must be eliminated. Staying alive for as long as possible is the order of the day. At first glance, the major threat appears to come from the numerous and eponymous asteroids that float with a deadly grace across the screen. Indeed, such is their awesome but delicate power that even the screen cannot contain them and as they disappear from one side of the television set, so they reappear at the other to continue their journey. However, to the seasoned pilot, the asteroids are but an incidental hazard. The true enemy are the enemy spacecraft as, where the space debris moves according to the laws of momentum, enemy ships are motivated and have both intelligence and purpose. Two types of enemy craft populate this infinite realm. The larger of them is comparatively easy to pick off but the smaller is devious and possesses a sentience that enables it to seek out the player's ship, predicting its trajectory and firing off missiles into which the hapless quarry all too often steers.

Videogames and space battles are inexorably linked. Many is the game that has pitted player against an oncoming horde in the lonely, black depths beyond the atmosphere. However, this is not merely an aesthetic decision, not simply a matter of outer space being exciting, untraversed and unexplored, not merely an extension of science fiction, the fear of the alien other or the projection of 1950s Futurism into the universe of interactivity. Rather, there are very practical reasons for videogames being set in the blackness of outer space. In fact, that it is black is perhaps more important than that it is space, as black is free in videogame technology terms. Black is

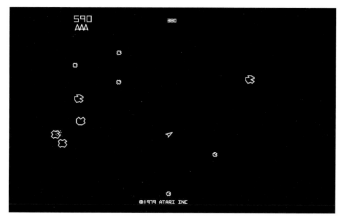

Asteroids: in space, no-one can hear you lurk

the colour of the unilluminated screen and in an era where graphics technology was limited, to say the least, drawing as little as possible was eminently desirable, if not essential. As such, games set against the featurelessness of space were commonplace as this required only the spaceships, starfields, missilefire and, in this case, asteroids, to be drawn. The remainder of the universe is taken care of in all its rigorously rendered detail by the drab, barren featurelessness of the blank screen. Atari attempted a similar strategy, though with a somewhat stretched conceit, in their 1976 *Night Driver* game that evaded the need for drawing complex scenery and roadside detail by simply shifting the driving to unlit highways and ensuring that the player only embarked on journeys in the dead of night. As such, it is interesting to note that the prevalence of space games then has less to do with the desire to evoke a specific aesthetic than it represents an inventive solution to the problem of gross technological limitation.

While the interstellar setting may have been a stroke of design genius and may have made the best of a limited technical palette, *Asteroids'* most significant contribution to the world of videogaming is altogether less intentional. Though not quite a design flaw, *Asteroids* does include one of the earliest exploitable design 'features'. In order to gain the highest scores, the player is well employed to 'lurk'. Lurking involves destroying all but one of the asteroids, thereby clearing the screen of obstacles and confusion, and waiting for the appearance of enemy spacecraft that may be shot down for large point bonuses. By leaving just a lone asteroid floating through the void and picking off the high-scoring ships, a player may, in theory at least, continue playing indefinitely.[4] However, in practice, whether lurking or 'playing fair', the player always loses in the end as one of the other consequences of *Asteroids* belonging to the old school of game design is that, like *Space Invaders* and *Defender*, the game's structure is infinite. That is, the game has no ultimate victory state; no denouement or climax in which the player is victorious. Rather, the game continues inexorably, becoming progressively harder and faster until the player succumbs to its pressures or simply decides that they can take no more. *Asteroids* pits the lone player against the combined evils of the rest of the universe in a potentially heroic manner but its message is ultimately a bleak one. Though you may enjoy the fight, you cannot win. You may even get to enter your initials on the high-score table, but this is a record only of the best losers, those that took longest to die. Every set of initials stands in memory of a fallen pilot not a victorious hero. Indeed, the blackness of *Asteroids*' spacescape is matched only by the tone of its underlying narrative. It is a blast, though.

4. By the sequel, *Asteroids Deluxe* (1980), 'lurking' had been outlawed with enemy ships smart enough to blast away the remaining asteroid fragments thereby ending the stage and forcing the player to progress with the game as intended.

Publisher: Atari; **Platform**: Coin-Op.

Batalyx
1985
Jeff Minter

***

As the personalities of individual designers have been mostly bred out of the videogame mass market over recent years – there are few videogame designers who have stamped their individuality on their work as consistently and as self-consciously as England's Jeff Minter. Minter's work is often characterised by the outward appearance of 'old'-school gameplay systems and conventions (more often than not the graceful shmup) wrapped inside a counter-culture aesthetic and posture that draws heavily on the cultural heritage of creative narcotics. The final, and most defining, layer to his signature style is the insistence of including ungulates as icons and characters in his work. Minter loves his 'beasties' and he intends to share that love with anyone who wants to play.

Minter delivers an uncompromising approach to game design, constantly driving forwards an increasing complexity of systems and intensity of visual design in a series of titles that while not always successful have always been consistent to his mission.

While not his most commercially successful title, *Batalyx* provides an introduction to the key interests of his work conveniently wrapped in a single title. As a primer in one of the most interesting game designers working today, it's an essential download. (Minter made the game public domain and it is now freely available to be played under emulation.) Minter called *Batalyx* a 'game-system' – a collection of six mini-games in one, which the player could swap between at any time during the time-limited gameplay. *Batalyx* has no 'lives', only time.

Batalyx is almost a greatest hits album – his gaming concerns today distilled down to their core concepts. For the populist, a wholly serviceable version of *Attack of the Mutant Camels* is included, the *Defender* clone that secured his reputation in its original release. For the experimental, the reflex-gaming of *The Activation of Iridis Base* dispenses with accessibility and the meditative *Synchro II* (with its beautiful sonic design) provides a unique, inertia-driven puzzle.

Perhaps most notable is the inclusion of the 'pause-mode' game. The clock stops when the player selects game #6, and a version of the virtual-light-synthesiser 'Psychadelia' fills the screen. The VLM work has been a core concern of his work over the years – the concept of a collaborative performance tool that allows groups of players to work together to create extraordinary hallucinogenic lightshows in response to music. The VLM has evolved exponentially in visual quality as hardware power has increased (the most recent version, 'Neon', is embedded into the Microsoft Xbox 360 hardware) and it is fascinating to revisit the origins of the VLM on an 8-bit machine.

Publisher: Llamasoft; **Platform**: Commodore 64/128.

Burnout 3: Takedown
2004
Criterion Games

With *Gran Turismo* declaring itself to be the most accurate high-performance driving simulation, labouring over the precise modelling of the physics and handling on the vehicles it featured, Criterion chose to plough a different approach. The *Burnout* series eschew precise simulation in pursuit of giving the player the impression that they are travelling as quickly and dangerously as possible.

Burnout is about excess. The original game introduced the basic premise, which rewards the player for dangerous driving. *Burnout 2* is considered by many to the best iteration. It built on the original with the addition of 'crash mode' wherein the player is challenged to cause as much damage as possible. The third version, however, was the title to finally achieve mass-market success – particularly in North America. *Burnout 3* gave the player the new challenge of 'takedowns', the wilful destruction of another car within the context of a race. The most remarkable characteristic of *Burnout*, though, is the abandon with which its core ideas have been exaggerated. The sense of speed felt within the game is peerless. The tromboning of the perspective lines when rapid acceleration occurs, the 'burn' lines of lights as they fly by you and the heavy motion-blur combine to create a visceral racing experience. The sensation is that of being propelled through the gameworld barely in control, a world where all the physical properties have been stretched to their most exciting point.

The signature feature in *Burnout 3* is its crashes. Whenever a takedown collision occurs the camera leaves the point of view of the player and snaps to a slow motion version of the unfolding destruction (although not always from the best camera vantage point). When the player finds themselves crashing, the same slow motion can be triggered and subtle amounts of 'aftertouch' can be added to the direction of the crashing vehicle. In this way the player can attempt to cause even more collisions by steering their out of control machine into the path of other cars. This celebratory fetishisation of the high-speed crash takes so much obvious joy in its brute physicality, one feels it would make even J. G. Ballard blush.

Criterion is rapidly emerging as a studio to be noted for their extremity. In the *Burnout* series they pushed the racing genre to an almost comedic sense of speed; more recently, with *Black*, they stretched the first-person shooter genre to an almost ridiculous level of destruction. Gamers have seldom travelled as fast.

Publisher: EA Games; **Platform**: Sony PlayStation 2, Microsoft Xbox.

Buzz: The Music Quiz
2005
Relentless Software

Partially through ubiquity, but far more so through innovation, the Sony PlayStation 2 has done more than any other electronic gaming device to open up videogames to the masses. The strategy hasn't been about translating existing titles to new audiences through sheer marketing and PR spend; rather it has been about aggressive innovation of new ideas.

Recognising that one of the principal barriers to the 'rest' of the family playing a videogame was the innate complexity of the dual-shock controller and its fourteen buttons (and two sticks), a core strategy has been to create new methods for player input. *EyeToy* removed the controller completely and let people use their bodies, *SingStar* gave people the microphone and bid them to perform – now *Buzz* gives players a big red button and asks them questions about pop music. Most importantly, it flashes like any quiz show button should.

A party game rapidly developed to ensure inclusion in a leading store's new catalogue, *Buzz* attempts to transfer the world of the Saturday night game-show to your front room. Supplied with four buzzers, the supporting marketing campaign demonstrated very little about what *Buzz* was – and everything about what a *great* party you could have if you played it. Like Trivial Pursuit or charades before it, *Buzz* is a tool for enabling fun with friends. You need only supply the beer, crisps and, of course, friends. This is not to be played alone.

The decision was made early on in the development to include the four buzzers as a separate peripheral precisely because of that party dynamic requirement. With the PS2 only supporting two controllers and few people owning a dual-tap expander, a separate controller device would be the only practical way to enable more than two people to play at once. The number of players and their active participation in the spirit of the game is crucial to the experience of *Buzz*. Intentionally, it leaves areas of the game reasonably sparse specifically to allow the people playing to create their own narrative. Extending into the living room, the game understands that the players are engaged in a social activity, and gives them the requisite space to argue, tease and compete. The game rounds are kept deliberately simple because its contestants will probably be slightly drunk. In its own way, it is following wholly the model prescribed by *EyeToy* and *SingStar* in transferring the performance over to the players. Like these titles, there is a direct link between the enjoyment of the game and the enthusiasm of the players.

Publisher: SCEE; **Platform**: Sony PlayStation 2.

Cannon Fodder
1983
Sensible Software

Few games have courted controversy quite as audaciously as this 1983 release from Jon Hare's Sensible Software. Videogames have long used military activities as the basis for gameplay (mainly shooting rather than, say, bridge-building) and while there have been notable examples where specific scenarios have been referenced (*1942*'s Pacific War), generally games have shied away from any direct commentary on war itself. It's not difficult to see why. The apparent triviality of the videogame as perceived by the popular media is somewhat at odds with the rather more sober nature of warfare and the mass loss of human life. One could be forgiven, then, for reading the subtitle of *Cannon Fodder*, 'War has never been so much fun', as something of a provocation. This, coupled with the explicit iconography of the corn poppy on the game's box art, and publishers Virgin Interactive were

Cannon Fodder: war has never been so much fun

well on the way to propagating a moral outcry. But *Cannon Fodder* stands as more than just a carefully constructed outrage for the purposes of selling more copies. The game is a genuine attempt at videogame satire, and as such is fraught with all of the tensions that any ironic exercise displays.

While making no attempt to create a photo-real representation of war, *Cannon Fodder* skilfully puts its miniature pixel soldiers through episodes of profoundly unpleasant (and often prolonged) agony and death. The screams of a small pixellated soldier as he slowly bleeds to death were particularly effective, both in exposing the game's commitment to its serious intent – and also in creating giggles of nervous laughter in the player. The game goes on to ram its message home in the queue of new intake soldiers waiting to start the game in front of a hill filled with graves and in the rapid list of the dead that is shown at the end of each level. All of the soldiers involved have names. The Royal British Legion themselves were outraged, particularly by the use of the poppy – but Sensible refused to compromise, adding a disclaimer to later versions of the title reading 'this game is not in any way endorsed by the Royal British Legion'.

Perhaps the greatest triumph of the game though, is that it completely delivers on its satiric agenda through the accomplished game design. The squad-based missions balance strategic advance with fast-action sequences incredibly well and in particular succeed in creating an interface free from the usual complexities of war-games. In many respects, *Cannon Fodder* is a fascinating forbearer of the 'news-games' of recent years – but placed awkwardly within a mass-market context. However unprepared or unwilling the cultural guardians of the time were to accept this for the sophisticated piece that it was, we should applaud Sensible for committing to even attempting something as complex as ironic social commentary within the fledgling form of the computer game. Ultimately, the entire construct would have collapsed had they not seduced players into enjoying themselves by delivering a game people enjoyed. War genuinely never had been this much fun.

Publisher: Virgin Interactive; **Platform**: Commodore Amiga.

Championship Manager
1992
Sports Interactive

Championship Manager is a true British success story. Created by two young brothers, Oliver and Paul Collyer, coding in their bedroom, it is the stuff of game development legend and there is a palpable sense of glee in their recollection of the difficulties encountered getting the game published. 'EA must be kicking themselves now . . . after they said they did not want to publish CM 1.'[5] From relatively humble beginnings, the series has gone on to become one of this country's most important sports games franchises and enjoys a fanatically loyal and committed fanbase who eagerly devour updated versions.

Yet, on the face of it, the game does not sound a particularly likely proposition. Unlike most other football games, in *Championship Manager* the actual matches, the ninety minutes of play, are relegated to relative insignificance. The twists and turns of individual fixtures, with their near-misses and wasted chances, open goals and penalty claims, are

Championship Manager: the beautiful game?

less important than the cumulative weight of a season's scores on team standings in leagues and cup competitions. In fact, the visual representation of matches is at best functional and symbolic with coloured markers standing in for the players showing little if any of the flair that marks out the 'beautiful game'. Moreover, for those overwhelmed even by this level of graphical spectacle, matches may be rendered solely as textual summaries. This utilitarian approach is not a consequence of the limitations of early games hardware. Certainly the Amiga and Atari ST were both capable machines in their own right and even in the most recent incarnations of the series available for graphical powerhouses like PlayStation Portable and Xbox 360, the visual representation of fixtures is functional to say the least.

The lack of graphical splendour may come as something of a surprise but more shocking still is the revelation that the *Championship Manager* player exerts no direct control over the way the action pans out on the pitch during matches. And so we find a videogame about football where the individual members of the team cannot be controlled by any amount of keyboard or joystick manipulation. This is not a football game. Rather, it is a videogame about football. It is a management simulator. Where series like Electronic Arts' *FIFA* or Konami's *Pro Evolution Soccer* offer their audience the opportunity to step into the boots of David Beckham or Wayne Rooney, *Championship Manager* has them donning a virtual camel coat and sits them in a pitch-side dugout. Essentially, this is virtualised implementation of a Fantasy Football League. However, there are important differences. Chief among them is the sheer complexity of the simulation of football management. There is much more to this business than simply selecting a team and letting them loose on the pitch. Even the earliest incarnation of *Championship Manager* demanded the would-be manager to juggle a huge number of variables for each player, arrange transfers and required a detailed knowledge of both football and business in general. Subsequent sequels have sought to add further complexity to the model such that current editions include overseas and youth training programmes, for example.

With matches but a small part of the game and ultimately recreated in the imagination rather than displayed on screen, the majority of a manager's time is spent poring over tables of statistics. As such, to the uninitiated, *Championship Manager* looks very much like a Microsoft *Excel* spreadsheet, albeit decorated in the colours of a favourite football team, and its density seems impenetrably intricate. However, passion for the game is immense and fansites abound via which managers share strategy and tactics. More unexpectedly, avid fans produce artwork and elaborate, highly personal narratives in which successful campaigns are recounted.[6]

Developer Sports Interactive and Eidos, who had published *Championship Manager 2* onward, parted company in 2005. Eidos retained the *Championship Manager* name and have continued to release games under the brand while Sports Interactive took their code and redesigned their game as *Football Manager*.

5. <www.sigames.com/softography.php?type=view&id=1>.
6. See <www.thedugout.net> for examples of *Championship Manager/Football Manager* fan fiction.

Publisher: Domark; **Platform**: Commodore Amiga, Atari ST.

Dance Dance Revolution
1998
Konami

For many years, critics of videogames have pointed to their potentially harmful effects. More often than not, concern has centred on the content of the games themselves and its ability to reinforce or suggest certain types of behaviour (see *Manhunt*, for example). However, even those who accept that the majority of videogames such as *Gran Turismo*, *Zoo Keeper* and *Lumines* are less problematic representationally and in terms of the activities they promote and allow the player to indulge in, the very fact that people are playing videogames at all is still troublesome. The fear centres on videogame play's contribution to the sedentary lifestyles of young people who are characterised as couch potatoes slumped in a near-catatonic stupor in front of their TV screens. No matter that letters to the *British Medical Journal* point to the fact that medical research makes no link between videogame play and childhood obesity;[7] the popular message remains clear, videogames are bad for your health.

One antidote to this way of thinking would be to watch a *Dance Dance Revolution* player for a few minutes. This game is hard work and while it may be most effective as part of a calorie-controlled diet, it is no sedentary pastime for couch potatoes. *Dance Dance Revolution* is part of Konami's growing stable of 'Beatmania' (or 'Bemani') games, but where titles such as *Guitar Freaks*, *DrumMania* and *Mambo A Go Go* ask the player to become part of the band as they perform as a guitarist or percussionist, *Dance Dance Revolution* pushes the musicians into the orchestra pit and brings on the dancing girls (and boys). *Dance Dance Revolution* is essentially a rhythm action game in much the same vein as the other titles in the Bemani genre and gameplay revolves around rhythmically performing to a pre-recorded soundtrack. Icons move across the screen dictating a rhythm that must be tapped out with as much accuracy and precision as the player can muster. The twist here is that there are no drums skins to beat, record decks to scratch or guitars to strum. Instead, the controller is a virtual stage and the medium of this performance is dance. The dancefloor consists of four pressure pads marked out with directional arrows: left, right, up and down. As corresponding arrow icons move down the screen, the player must rhythmically tap the corresponding floorpad with their feet, thereby performing a choreographed routine in time with the music. It all sounds remarkably simple and, like many of the most enduring game designs, it is a fundamentally uncomplicated concept, but it requires considerable concentration and co-ordination, not to mention a good degree of physical stamina. The variability of tempi both between tracks and, most importantly, within individual pieces of music, adds to the complexity of the experience and will have all but the most experienced dancers in a tangle and gasping for breath as they try to recover from a 300 bpm workout. Multiplayer modes allow players to indulge their *Strictly Come Dancing* fantasies and battle side-by-side with a friend or rival.

Such is the popularity of *Dance Dance Revolution* that it has spawned many iterations with new music to perform to while leaving the basic gameplay relatively untouched. For those too shy to strut their stuff in public, or for those wishing to practise their routines before taking them on the road, *Dance Dance Revolution* has been ported to most current-generation home consoles. Most critically, a range of dancemats, from those that fold up for easy storage or to hide one's embarrassment to substantial metal-framed stages like those found in the arcade cabinet, are available. In fact, the dancemat is becoming inescapable. Not only are they in our arcades and homes, but they are even making their way into schools as part of physical education classes.[8] Who said videogames are bad for your health?

7. For more, see M. Griffiths (2005).
8. 'US pupils to dance themselves fit'. BBC News Online, Friday, 27 January 2006. Available at <news.bbc.co.uk/1/hi/technology/4653434.stm>.

Publisher: Konami; **Platform**: Coin-Op.

Deus Ex
2000
Ion Storm Austin

Emerging from the Austin branch of development studio Ion Storm (founded by *DOOM* co-creator John Romero and made infamous by his high-profile vanity-project commercial disaster *Daikatana*) *Deus Ex* was created by a relatively small team of twenty people over some three years. While having the external appearance of a first-person shooter and clearly influenced by seminal titles such as *Half-Life*, *Deus Ex* differs from the countless 'me-too' first-person shooter (FPS) genre cash-ins in that it is the product of Ion Storm's commitment to a radical manifesto for progressing the form. Indeed, the audacity of ambition is such that it is remarkable that it achieved as much as it did.

Deus Ex is an exhilarating and occasionally bewildering fusion of gameplay systems and genre conventions. An attempt to create an entirely open-gameworld – a sandbox for the player to explore – had, of course, been employed before and certainly has been since; *Deus Ex*'s innovation was to attempt to weld this open form with a complex, literate and responsive narrative. Warren Spector, the project director, claimed it was an attempt to treat the player as a collaborator – to create a gameworld that would allow the player to express themselves as freely as possible, take whatever actions they liked and then deal with the consequences. A detailed and growing set of design rules were constructed such as 'problems will have multiple solutions', 'locations will be reachable in several ways' and 'combat will require more thought than "What's the biggest gun in my inventory?" ' Indeed, it is possible to complete the entire game without using any deadly weapons.

The game was an attempt to render the game designers and the conceit of their 'game' as invisible as possible during the playing of it. Players were invited to find their own individual solutions to problems that they encounter on the journey towards their goal. This was a radically different proposition to the 'puzzle' model, where the player was charged with working out what the designers were thinking when they designed it. Spector was oft quoted as saying that there were no puzzles in the game, only problems.

The fun that the game delivers is in no small part delivered by its narrative context. In offering the player a 'real-world' causality in which actions have consequences, the designers wisely recognised that domestic present-day reality is a less than compelling context for a videogame. The 'reality' that players recognise in the game wasn't created through sophisticated physics modelling or through spectacular art design, but through more fundamental cues. While *Deus Ex* plays out wholly at night in a dystopian cyberpunk world, weaving the player through labyrinthine conspiracy theories – there is an ever present system of human common-sense. Objects and characters within the game are all invested with a tangible function and behave exactly as one might expect

Deus Ex: what's the biggest gun in my inventory?

them to – hence the absence of any telephones.

Ironically, the extraordinary density of the story and the level of detail afforded to every nuance within it in some respects works against the game. Clearly some years ahead of its time, it was almost difficult to trust that the apparent influence and freedom gifted to the player within it was actually real. In wearing its complexity on its sleeve and refusing to patronise the player, it made an extraordinary push into a new kind of gameplay that arguably hasn't been matched since. More than anything else, *Deus Ex* is a working example that player immersion in a world isn't contingent on photo-real graphical representation, but on intelligent and progressive design.

Publisher: Eidos Interactive; **Platform**: PC.

Donkey Kong
1981
Nintendo

If one were searching for the archetypal 'platform game', then *Donkey Kong* would be towards if not at the top of the list. Not only is it one of the first of this type of game, but also it is among the most literal implementations of the genre. Coming at this early stage in the maturation of this category of game, and indeed the videogame form as a whole, its platforms are just that – platforms. It is not that they lack the graphical prowess that would come with later, higher-powered technology, but rather that the world is actually comprised of construction materials. Metal girders linked together with ladders form the barest of structures. It is as though the foundations of what would become the most prevalent genre of the 1980s and early 1990s are being laid and the scaffolding that will shore up the next decade of videogaming is being erected. And taking these first steps is Mario. Still called 'Jumpman' at this stage, reflecting his definition solely in terms of

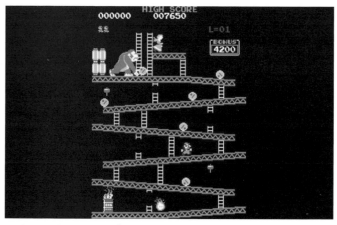

Donkey Kong: how high can you get?

capability rather than personality, *Donkey Kong* gave the world its first glimpse of a character who would go on to be more widely recognised than Mickey Mouse and would symbolise videogaming itself.

In keeping with the simplistic, binary world of 1980s videogames, if Mario/Jumpman is the hero then Donkey Kong must be the villain of the piece. Sure enough, the great ape has captured Pauline, Jumpman's belle, and so the fairy-tale rescue narrative that will become the staple of so many of the *Super Mario* games that follow is established at this early stage.

The gameplay is simple enough to describe. Having captured Pauline, Donkey Kong stands atop of series of platforms hurling barrels at anybody foolish enough to try to rescue the damsel in distress. As Jumpman/Mario, the player's task is to ascend the heights, jumping the barrels as they fall, to retrieve their love. No sooner has the player successfully reached the platform on which Pauline stands than she is whisked off by Kong to another, higher, part of the construction site. Subsequent levels involve removing pins from the platform structure so as to send Kong plummeting to the ground below and leaving the coast clear for the rescue bid. However, while the game is easy to describe, it is somewhat more difficult to execute given the relatively unforgiving nature of the collision detection system that sees the slightest contact with the falling barrels, and the precision required to pull off jumps and daring dashes to victory.

The seeds of platform gaming can be noted in *Donkey Kong* and although subsequent Shigeru Miyamoto-designed games would expand the vocabulary of the form by adding larger worlds to explore, the fundamental mechanic of a virtual obstacle course is evident here. This is a game in which almost everything is hostile and in which the environment itself, the platform and ladder, is part of the puzzle and challenge of the game, as well as forming a piece of the solution.

All of which, of course, leaves just one question. Why '*Donkey*' *Kong*? As Sheff (1993), Kent (2001) and Kohler (2005) note, there are many theories attempting to explain this seemingly bizarre name. Chief among them is that Nintendo, either by stealth or through a misheard or mistranslated conversation, sought to trade on the kudos and popularity of *King Kong*. Certainly the similarity in the two names was not missed by Universal Studios who, in 1982, attempted to sue Nintendo of America for copyright infringement. When it transpired that Universal did not own the rights to *King Kong* that it thought it did, the judgment went in Nintendo's favour. Accepted wisdom states the game's designer, Miyamoto, had no intention of naming the character/game 'Monkey Kong', but rather chose the word donkey to convey the stubbornness of the character.

Although appearing as a villain in this first game, Donkey Kong became the hero as the tables turned in the sequel in which Mario had kidnapped Kong's son. Subsequently, Donkey Kong and his family have become stalwarts of the *Super Mario* universe appearing in *Super Mario Kart* and being rejuvenated in their own *Donkey Kong Country* series of platform games released throughout the 1990s for the Super Nintendo Entertainment System (SNES).

Publisher: Nintendo; **Platform**: Coin-Op.

Donkey Konga
2004
Namco

In many ways, *Donkey Konga* is not revolutionary. It does not push back the boundaries of the genre to any great extent in that it does not advance the structure, design or play mechanic and, in fact, borrows heavily from the modalities of the form as established in games such as *PaRappa the Rapper*. It does not even introduce new characters and draws on Nintendo's extensive back catalogue of intellectual property.

Certainly, *Donkey Konga* is a more than competent rhythm action game with a characteristically well-designed front-end menu system and functional, if not lavish, in-game graphics. However, in a marketplace that had already witnessed the extraordinary charm of *PaRappa* and *Vib Ribbon*, one could be easily forgiven for dismissing Nintendo's effort as an also-ran. Of course, great videogames, like any works of art, do not necessarily need to be revolutionary and may earn their status through perfection or elegance in execution and implementation, although in the face of this apparent derivativeness it may surprise us to find that *Donkey Konga* received an award for innovation at the 2005 Game Developers Choice awards.[9]

Before any thoughts of corruption or the bribing of judges enter our minds, it should be noted that *Donkey Konga* is an absolutely deserving recipient of the accolade. The key is not too look for innovation on the screen. This is a game that is almost exclusively defined in terms of its hardware interface. Where *PaRappa the Rapper* takes the standard PlayStation controller and turns it into a virtual instrument, *Donkey Konga* goes one step further with a set of bongos to plug into the console. It is possible to play *Donkey Konga* with a standard GameCube controller but it becomes a wholly different experience. This is not a situation where the hardware interface merely improves or enhances gameplay as a force-feedback steering wheel might for *Gran Turismo*, for example. *Donkey Konga*'s 'DK Bongos' peripheral makes rhythm action both visceral and primal. As players beat their way through the selection of tunes, there is a real connection with the music that renders control via a standard controller distant and detached. In addition to the two skins, the kits include a microphone and players are required to clap as well as strike and roll the drums. The coup de grâce, however, is the multiplayer mode. Although the game is supplied with just one set of bongos, it supports the use of up to four sets simultaneously. The sight of four drummers beating and clapping along, either in competition or collaboration but always with a joyous abandon, ensures that *Donkey Konga* ranks among the finest party games – sociable, silly and, above all, fun.

In some of its mini-games, *Donkey Konga* hints at an interesting direction that Nintendo would explore in more depth with 2005's *Donkey Kong Jungle Beat*. Here, the DK Bongos are used to control the central character in a platform game: pounding left and right to move Donkey Kong, both to jump, and clapping to trigger context-sensitive special moves. Nintendo have also released two sequels to *Donkey Konga* that have left the fundamental gameplay unchanged but have added new musical tracks to hammer along to.

9. <www.gamechoiceawards.com/archive/gdca_5th.htm>.

Publisher: Nintendo; **Platform**: Nintendo GameCube.

DOOM
1993
id Software

Such was the furore that greeted *DOOM* in 1993 that the sustained
revulsion generated by the mainstream cultural commentators upon
release has established it as a convenient shorthand for everything that is
bad about videogames. While *Grand Theft Auto* inspires its own notable
level of disapproval, it has never quite managed to mine the depths of
id's seminal 1993 first-person shooter. It would be easy to think that the
most important thing about *DOOM* was the ease with which it ushered
in a new age of intensity in videogame violence, but to rest on that
assumption would be to ignore some of the more important and equally
influential ideas and innovations it pioneered.

While by no means the first first-person shooter, *DOOM* is assured its
place in gaming history not just by being excellently designed, but by
rapidly attaining a level of ubiquity made possible only by the new
distribution model it embraced, the Internet. id Software, following on
the success of their previous titles, *Wolfenstein* and *Commander Keen,*
had generated an extraordinary level of anticipation around the title –
and on 10 December 1993, *DOOM* was first uploaded onto the FTP
server of the University of Wisconsin. The game was the first to bring the
concept of 'shareware' to a true critical mass. The original download
offered players a limited but fully playable version of the game, on the
principle that they would then pay a fee to upgrade to the full version.
Since release, it is estimated that around 10 million downloads of the
original *DOOM* have been installed – and while not all of those were
upgraded to full versions, the viral nature of its distribution ensured a
solid foundation for sequels (which were not released as shareware).

DOOM casts the player as a Space Marine who, whilst deported to
Mars, finds himself in the unenviable position of being the last human
left alive when a series of portals are opened up allowing demons from
Hell to overrun the base. Placed solidly behind a variety of weapons

(ranging from shotgun to chainsaw to 'BFG') the player is challenged to fight their way back to Earth. The graphical innovations, pioneered by lead programmer John Romero, were extraordinary not just in their fidelity but because they were acutely focused on serving the intensity of that particular title. Rather than attempting to reach towards photo-realism in some broad 'cinematic' sense, the *DOOM* engine is dedicated only to creating the more immersive experience of the intensity of *DOOM* itself. To that end, Carmack delivered a generous service. For the first time, the players' weapon, visible at the foot of the screen, moved from side to side as they ran through the space. The player felt less like a fixed camera moving down a corridor, but an urgent, rushed character sprinting around a chaotic world. The complex level design, principally driven by John Carmack, makes great use of the new capabilities the engine affords it. The arenas no longer exist as perpendicular grids of walls. Corridors twist and turn, floors and ceilings comprise moving levels – spatial puzzles are afforded a greater complexity than previously possible.

The level structure for *DOOM*, in an astute commercial committed strategy, was made open to any players who wanted to construct their own levels, which would run within it. A number of level editors would be released, allowing players to create WAD files that would run within the *DOOM* engine. Tens of thousands of modifications ('mods') of *DOOM* would be released with a huge variety of different subjects. Mostly unlicensed fan tributes to sci-fi and action-movie brands, *DOOM* would also host 'Simpsons DOOM' and 'Marine DOOM' – officially created by the US Marine Corp.

DOOM is also acutely aware of the atmospheric power of darkness. Whereas previous titles had only offered one brightness level across entire worlds, *DOOM* allowed the highlighting of specific areas through differentiated lighting. Most importantly, the game thrust the player into disorientating darkness at key stages, forcing them to begin to orientate themselves by dim door signs and to identify the location of the enemies purely through the stereo depiction of their grunts.

One of the central innovations *DOOM* tabled was to allow easy network play over Ethernet; thus, any player could fight against (or indeed, collaborate with) their colleagues over the local area network. More often than not, those networks were the ones at places of work or education – causing several high-profile institutions such as Intel and Carnegie Mellon University to create anti-*DOOM* policies for their intranets. The 'deathmatch' was to become a core component of the first-person shooter genre forever and *DOOM* would cement its place as one of the principal causes of loss of productivity in the world's corporate workforce.

Publisher: id Software; **Platform**: PC.

Dr Kawashima's Brain Training
2006
Nintendo

With UK advertising directed explicitly at the hitherto undiscovered 'grey' market, this radical title from Nintendo set itself lofty goals. Rather than focusing on expanding the audience for handheld gaming, it sought to expand the entire perceived usage of the device. Rather than attempting to translate Mario and the Mushroom Kingdom to older audiences, Nintendo translated the device itself. The mainstream coverage that *Brain Training* achieved in the United Kingdom was almost without precedent. Sunday supplements, television news programmes, broadsheets were all co-opted into the revelatory story that videogames might have some tangible, sustainable and provable benefits for our mental health. Nintendo weren't building on an existing grey-gamer market; to all intents and purposes they were creating it from nothing. Here was a product that, for £20, slowed the onset of potential senility.

Like a number of titles that immediately preceded it, notably *Animal Crossing* and *Nintendogs*, *Brain Training* is a product with which the user builds a continuing relationship. Previously, this structured returning to a game might have been driven by unfolding narrative tension or an elusive high score. Here, it was driven by the calendar. *Brain Training* presents the user with a schedule and tracks their progress, presenting their progress back to them as they spend more and more time with the ebullient Dr Kawashima. Within a few days, one finds oneself with a close bond to the software. It knows if you miss a day, it congratulates you if you play well, it scolds you if you play too late at night – through the simple reading of the internal clock of the DS and the calendar, this recent series of games delivers a sensation of friendly intimacy. The Holy Grail surely for any product such as this, it becomes your friend. You're playing it for your own good.

While some editorial coverage poured scorn on the 'real' value of the software as a device to improve intelligence, the indisputable truth is that

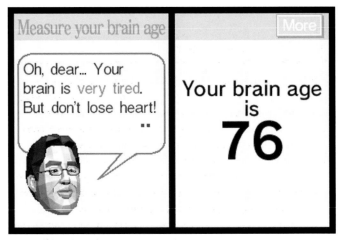

Dr Kawashima's Brain Training: Dr K breaks the news gently

a software product exists on a mainstream commercial gaming platform that is engaging people in performing rapid mental arithmetic for fun. As the software presents your achievements back to you in a friendly graph across a calendar, it's very difficult not to trust the methodologies it uses.

In so many respects, *Brain Training* feels almost like a reversal to the earliest days of Sinclair and Commodore home computers. When they first arrived in living rooms parents rubbed their hands with delight that finally something had arrived that would make learning fun, help children with their homework and engage them in all manner of worthy cerebral activities. When the games arrived and home computers became an evil distraction from their homework, the horror set in. Nintendo appear to have pulled off an extraordinary inversion of this. A handheld gaming machine, designed to be used as a time-filling distraction in spare moments has repurposed itself into a true personal computer. It'll be your friend, it'll make you feel good about your achievements and it'll make you smarter.

Publisher: Nintendo; **Platform**: Nintendo DS.

Dragon's Lair
1983
Advanced Microcomputer Systems

It simply looked *so* different. In the context of the arcades of the early 1980s where players were used to seeing purely pixel-based representations of characters, *Dragon's Lair* stood out like a wholly different kind of machine – and it was. The game was the first of any note to employ new laserdisc technology and was heralded as ushering in a new era of 'interactive movies', a phrase that has sadly stayed with us to this day.

Worked on by Hollywood animator Don Bluth, the game came with cinematic credentials and qualities pre-installed. The narrative concerned the adventures of Dirk the Daring and his efforts to rescue Princess Daphne from the eponymous lair of Singe the dragon. Bluth created the character designs in his trademark style and the attract mode of the game was much like watching a short Don Bluth movie. The experience of playing it was much the same.

Essentially a progression along a tree-structure of connected scenes, the player's interaction was limited to either choosing a direction or swinging his sword at the correct moment – which would trigger the 'success' animation. Whilst the animation was accomplished, the level of agency the player actually has in the game is incredibly limited. It's almost like the inverse of more recent titles such as *Prince of Persia: The Sands of Time*, where the player is made to feel as if they have extraordinary acrobatic skills with minimal effort – *Dragon's Lair* makes the player feel like they are bystanders, occasionally called upon to jog the story forward.

However, the game was a massive success; so much so that most of the laserdisc players in the original machines buckled under the pressure of so many repeated plays. Assured its place in gaming lore forever through sheer force of difference, *Dragon's Lair* is perhaps best remembered as a startling technology demonstration; an experiment exploring the difficult relationship between the concepts of 'interactive' and 'movie'.

Publisher: Cinematronics; **Platform**: Coin-Op.

Ecco the Dolphin
1992
Novotrade

Faced with the task of creating a videogame about dolphins, the cheap and easy solution would be to position man as the enemy. Polluted seas, disappearing habitats, even the ravages of unfriendly tuna nets all offer themselves as scenarios, enemies and obstacles. Cheap and easy perhaps, but all rather too obvious for a developer determined to swim against the tide. With *Ecco the Dolphin*, Novotrade set the adventure wholly beneath the ocean with not even the slightest recognition of man, let alone any battle against his environmental tyranny. The world conjured up is one of extraordinary depth, sumptuousness and colour as a labyrinth of subaquatic caverns filled with coral and crustaceans stretches out before the player. The backstory is utterly preposterous but at the same time strangely charming in its naiveté. Ecco has become separated from his pod, which was literally sucked out of the water by a mysterious storm. Our lone cetacean hero's task is to travel the oceans of the world to find his family and uncover the secret of the winds. To do so, he not only puzzles and explores his way through the undersea mazes of sprawling levels, but must also commune with a host of sea creatures, including dolphins from other pods from whom he learns the art of echolocation and even time travel. It transpires that man is wholly inconsequential in Ecco's story and any fear that global climate change or el Nino may be to blame are dispelled as the source of the disruption is traced back to the actions of an alien race many millions of years ago. There is definitely something of the summer of '67 about *Ecco the Dolphin*. We used to take it upon ourselves to save the whales, now the dolphins are saving us all.

In essence, *Ecco the Dolphin* is a platform game just like the myriad platform games that saturated the MegaDrive's catalogue throughout the 1990s. Of course, this statement comes with one caveat as there are no platforms in this game, but it must be remembered that mammals with no legs have little need for such things. With this difference aside, *Ecco*'s basic game mechanic and structure borrows heavily from the dominant genre of the age and it does it in an unremitting way. This is a devilishly hard game with unforgiving puzzles, dastardly time and air limits (don't forget, dolphins are mammals and need to surface to breathe) and, even accepting the infinite tries that the player is presented with, much of the time is spent despairing at the absurd difficulty level. What sets it apart from its brethren is its non-violent ethic and the quite incredible sense of being a dolphin – something that no game has ever captured so successfully (though, to be fair, none bar the sequels have ever tried). *Ecco* is about pressing onward in search of the goal, pressing onward to save one's family, one's species, one's world. It is absolutely not about racking up kills or wallowing in destruction. In hindsight, *Ecco the Dolphin* marks the calm before the storm, and sits in stark contrast to wanton bloodletting of games such as *Mortal Kombat* that kicked and punched their way onto the MegaDrive the following year.

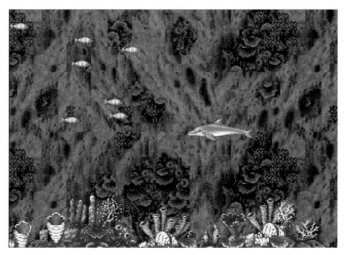

Ecco the Dolphin: I hope these fish are dolphin friendly

Above, or perhaps that should be beneath, it all, *Ecco the Dolphin* is a game about control. The experience is truly serene as player and mammal become one, brought together through the unlikely conduit of a black, plastic, three-buttoned controller. Indeed, such is the feeling of oneness with the gameworld that this is one of those few occasions when an otherwise tired videogaming cliché is wholly appropriate. *Ecco the Dolphin*'s controls are fluid.

Publisher: Sega; **Platform**: Sega MegaDrive.

Electroplankton
2005
Nintendo

According to its creator, renowned media artist Toshio Iwai, *Electroplankton* is 'what happens when you combine a microscope, a tape recorder, a synthesizer, and an NES'.[10] In publicity materials, Nintendo call it 'Touchable media art'. Whatever we call it, however preposterous or pretentious, can we call it a videogame? It has no winning or losing state, though you can certainly perform well or badly and, aside from creating music, it has no objective per se, but then neither does *The Sims*. *Electroplankton* belongs to that group of titles that challenges our definitions of game, toy and videogame almost to breaking point. Nevertheless, there can be no doubt that *Electroplankton* has been designed to be played – or perhaps to be played *with* – and, unlike many experimental experiences that self-consciously push at the boundaries of 'game', this works. And it is fun.

Electroplankton is a music and media experience. In 'Audience mode', it is essentially a semi-random jukebox. Where the game comes into its own, however, is in 'Performance mode' where the player interacts with a unique species of miniscule sea-dwelling plankton that can be coaxed into producing music through stylus, clapping and voice commands. Ten types of electroplankton can be selected each with their own particular music-making ability. 'Tracy' plankton, for example, swim along lines drawn by the player's stylus; 'Rec-Rec' capture, loop and process microphone input, such as the player's voice; and, in typically self-referential style, 'Beatnes' allow sequences to be constructed using samples and effects from classic Nintendo game soundtracks.

Importantly, there is little precision offered in *Electroplankton*'s performance interface. The various plankton environments present no equivalents of piano keyboards, staffs or other such familiar musical input or notation devices. Instead, the music is largely freeform and abstract, though the repertoire never quite veers into the experimental discordance of Stockhausen and is perhaps closer to John Cage's 'chance music' in its apparent randomness. Certainly, in eschewing traditional videogame elements like high scores, winning and losing, *Electroplankton* seems to share something of Cage's Zen-inspired sense of 'purposeless play'. Tonally, the bell-like timbres of some of the plankton lend *Electroplankton* music a decidedly new-age feel and it frequently takes on the hypnotic, meditative quality of windchimes.

Like *Yoshi Touch & Go*, *WarioWare Touched!* and *Trauma Center*, *Electroplankton* provides further evidence of the innovation that Nintendo's DS handheld has fostered. While Sony's PSP plays host to games such as *Lumines* that make excellent use of sound as well as graphics, the tactility and immediacy that the DS affords through its touch screen interface creates a connection that buttons and switches cannot match, while the microphone allows the player to personalise their experience by literally placing themselves within the soundscape by recording their voice – or any sound for that matter.

Electroplankton has been criticised in some quarters for its lack of a save or archiving feature. While this ephemerality may be consistent with the somewhat wistful nature of the plankton themselves, that the performances are unrepeatable can be undeniably irritating and certainly prohibits the sharing of the often surprisingly rich musical output. Some fans, however, have refused to let their masterworks disappear when the batteries run out or the DS lid closes and a community sharing mp3 files of *Electroplankton* tunes thrives online.

10. *Electroplankton* instruction booklet, Nintendo, 2005: 57.

Publisher: Nintendo; **Platform**: Nintendo DS.

Elite
1984
David Braben and Ian Bell

Elite is a space-trading game set over eight galaxies, giving thousands of planets to explore. The overall aim of the game is to develop one's player ranking to a level of 'elite', after beginning the game ranked as 'harmless' with just a hundred credits. The open-ended structure of the game allows progress to be made through legal or illegal means – introducing the device of moral choice into the videogame world. The game takes place within a first-person view of the player's cockpit, from which the rest of space is rendered in animated 3D wireframe graphics.

Upon its release in 1984, *Elite* was priced at £12.99. With most games priced at around £7.99 or less, this was an audaciously high price for a home computer game and signalled the ambition and pretensions of the game. The sense of grandeur and scale was compounded in the packaging with a bulging shrink-wrapped box containing copious manuals, star charts, stickers and a specially commissioned novella by sci-fi author Robert Holdstock to accompany the game itself.

For all its Kubrick-esque 'space opera' sensibilities, *Elite* was ostensibly a buy-low, sell-high trading game based around simple transactions. The game's principal innovation was to grant the player a new feeling of boundless freedom. This was generated not only by the spatial dimensions offered by the more than 2,000 planets available, but also by a moral freedom afforded to the player. Players could choose to live by fair trade, by bounty hunting, by operating as a pirate or any combination of the three – with all choices having an effect on their relationship with the law enforcement community of the galaxy. In doing so, it prefigured the kinds of freedoms and the ethical frameworks that were to become vogue in later titles such as *Black and White* and *Grand Theft Auto*.

The memory limitations of the BBC Micro meant that the galaxies and planet names in *Elite* were generated by algorithm. It being impossible to check all of the generated names, mild embarrassment for the makers ensued when a player discovered a planet named 'Arse' in one of the unchecked galaxies (Spufford, 2003: 114).

The visual style of *Elite* was also remarkable, bringing the 3D wireframe graphics of *Battlezone* and *Star Wars*, previously only seen in an arcade, to a home computer system for the first time. In turn, this lay the path for titles such as *Starglider* and *Mercenary*. The combat system in *Elite* built very effectively on the radar innovation of *Defender* by creating a small 3D 'scanner' in the centre of the players' display. The sense of tangible scale and immersion this generated was incredibly effective.

Coded by Ian Bell and David Braben, two undergraduates at Jesus College, Cambridge, *Elite* represents one of the high-water marks of the 'bedroom coder' age. Eventually going on to sell 150,000 copies on the BBC Micro (a ratio of 1:1) *Elite* went on to be reissued on all major platforms and continues to be developed as a franchise by David Braben. Braben and Bell's working relationship deteriorated in the years following the initial release, and Bell has not been involved in any of the subsequent sequels.

Publisher: Acornsoft; **Platform**: BBC Micro.

EyeToy: Play
2003
Sony London Studios

'With *EyeToy*, you are the controller.' So proclaims the video instruction manual that accompanies Sony's most innovative contribution to videogaming. It sounds like science fiction. It sounds like it won't work. But it isn't. And it does. And it is fun.

For all the talk of change and development in the videogames industry and the constant fetishisation of imminent release that immediately renders obsolete the current generation of games and platforms, it is sobering to remember that some things have not changed in decades. The videogame controller has gone through a fair number of refinements and revisions, with joysticks falling from favour and being replaced by joypads and the sheer number of switches multiplying with each new console, but

Eye Toy: Play: come and have a go if you think you're hard enough

fundamentally the device has survived unaltered since the 1980s. A directional pad or stick controls the basic movement of a character, ship or other avatar, while switches and buttons simulate the performance of triggers, accelerators or brakes or make a character jump. All this would change in 2003 when Sony unveiled *EyeToy: Play*. This was no minor adjustment or recalibration of the basic controller model but a complete overhaul that boldly discarded everything videogame ergonomics engineers had learned about hardware design. Making use of a simple webcam, *EyeToy*'s genius was that it turned the player's body into a controller allowing gestural input. And so, in one fell swoop, flailing arms about became a legitimate part of the language of videogame play. It is difficult to express just how liberating *EyeToy* is, or how much fun it is to play with.

EyeToy: Play was the first title to support the camera peripheral, though there have been many more that either require the camera (such as *EyeToy Play: 2* and *3*; *Groove*; and *AntiGrav*) or that can take advantage of it to provide additional features such as capturing the player's picture for inclusion in the game (including *Buzz* and *SingStar*). The first *EyeToy: Play* offered twelve mini-games that involved washing windows, spinning plates and karate-chopping enemies. Subsequent titles have evolved the form and include simultaneous multiplayer options, while *EyeToy: Kinetic* offers a full workout training regime so you can keep fit and have fun at the same time.

Of course, because *EyeToy: Play* is so inherently accessible and requires little introduction and no a priori knowledge of videogame interfaces and their conventions, this fun is open to a far wider audience than most games. It is no accident that Sony's promotional materials and packaging for the first *EyeToy: Play* feature a diverse cross-section of players. Indeed, the introductory video shows *EyeToy* being set up and played by a kindly looking, grey-haired granny. This is audience widening writ large.

What is so interesting about *EyeToy: Play* is that the player gets to see just how much fun they are having as they see themselves on screen. Their own smiling face beams back at them reinforcing the pleasure.

Moreover, the player is literally placed in the virtual world. *EyeToy*'s most fascinating and innovative feature is not the way it takes the player's body and turns it into a controller, but rather the way it incorporates the physical space of the living room and makes it part of the gameworld. Surrounded by computer-generated characters and scenery, there is a real sense of presence in the world, with genuine sensations of control and also, unexpectedly, of touch and feel. Despite the lack of haptic feedback, hitting an object in an *EyeToy: Play* game has a solidity that blurs the distinction between real and virtual in a manner that *Virtual Reality* rarely managed. Not bad for £30.

Publisher: Sony Computer Entertainment Europe; **Platform**: Sony PlayStation 2.

Fahrenheit
2005
Quantic Dream

At least it fully commits to what it's trying to be, it really does. There's no doubting the intentions of auteur developer David Cage in the development of his thriller *Fahrenheit*. There is absolutely no doubting the utter earnestness of his attempt to make something entirely unique for you. Even down to his own appearance in the tutorial for the game, Cage is willing to put his name and reputation on the line for what the game is trying to do. In pre-release interviews, Cage was adamant that this was a new type of game. So much so, that it actually wasn't a game, it was an 'interactive film'. Indeed, the developer's site claims, 'Quantic Dream is the inventor of the Interactive Cinema format. *Fahrenheit* is the first project to be developed in this format.' It was with that phrase that suspicions were first raised.

The game is undeniably stylish. Its visual design displays a deep understanding of contemporary genre cinema and television. In particular, the game references *24* (or maybe *The Thomas Crown Affair*?) in its use of split-screen narrative to engineer suspense. The soundtrack and sonic design of the game also contribute well towards its aspirations of creating that specific mood of the cinematic thriller. Even in the performances of the voice actors and the maturity (albeit within the *X-Files*-esque genre) of the script it holds its own well. In fact, if *Fahrenheit* were an episode of the *X-Files* it would be moderately entertaining. As it stands, it exposes better than any other project since *Dragon's Lair* the fundamental tensions at the heart of the interactive film project.

Playing *Fahrenheit* is much like trying to watch a film, but with someone distracting you constantly. Unfortunately in this case, the distraction is interactivity. Unlike other titles – which reference cinematic action-cinema archetypes (*Half-Life 2*, *God of War*), cinematic narrative cliché (*The Secret of Monkey Island*) or even cinematic pomposity (*Metal Gear Solid*) – *Fahrenheit* attempts to fully straddle this divide between the linear and the interactive with its bold claims. In some sections it would be possible to argue that this works. Particularly in some of the action sequence where the user is required, 'simon'-like, to repeat the controller movements that are shown on screen, one is directly influencing an apparently more complex action on screen. This isn't any fun.

It's ultimately almost heart-breaking to play it, as the volume of effort that has gone into the title is so palpable from playing it. The game believes so, so much in what it is you feel yourself willing it to work, desperately wanting someone to make a convincing case for 'interactive cinema'. But it doesn't arrive. *Fahrenheit* is a tremendously important set of questions and should be experienced. Is it a game? Is it a film?

No.

Publisher: Atari; **Platform**: Microsoft Xbox, Sony PlayStation 2, Windows PC.

Fantavision
2000
Sony Computer Entertainment Inc.

Throughout 1999, Sony's marketing machine began to whip up excitement for its forthcoming PlayStation 2 console. Where the original PlayStation had brought 3D into the home and even made games cool with titles like *WipEout*, PS2 heralded an era of 'emotional gaming'. Complex narratives, detailed characters and filmic allusions were the watchwords of this new generation – Sony even sexed up the otherwise dull components of the system so what used to be called a 'graphics processing unit' was now the 'Emotion Engine'. Pre-release footage of titles such as Square-Enix's *The Bouncer* indicated that games were not simply growing up, but that they were transforming into rich media experiences – so exciting was the next-generation proposition that journalists and marketers even dusted off the phrase 'interactive movies'.

That the revolution was exaggerated would have surprised few with any experience of the games market. However, finding *Fantavision* among the few titles available at the European launch of PS2 was a surprise even for sceptics. A puzzle game based around detonating sequences of brightly coloured fireworks was about as far from Sony's next-generation promises as was possible to imagine – the 'oohs' and 'ahhs' of the fireworks display was not the emotional gaming players had hoped for. Not only did *Fantavision* not scream 'next generation', it was not even clear why it could not have been launched for the original PlayStation. Though its use of visual effects makes for an undeniably pretty, if not lavish, spectacle of vapour trails and incandescent explosions, it was not a graphically sophisticated game, nor did it make use of sound or controls in innovative ways. As such, far from making a noisy bang heralding the coming of a new age of gaming, *Fantavision* was largely passed over by players and disappeared with the familiar and disappointing whimper of a back-garden Catherine wheel that failed to go off.

However, this is all rather unfair. Had *Fantavision* not been elevated to the status of standard-bearer for the Sony's overblown PS2 aspirations, it might have enjoyed both critical and commercial success as it is, in fact, an accomplished, polished and rewarding game. In the tradition of great puzzle games like *Tetris* or, more recently, *Meteos* and *Lumines*, *Fantavision*'s objective is extremely simple. Fireworks of various colours are automatically launched from the bottom of the screen and the player is charged with detonating them before they fizzle out and fade to nothing. However, fireworks can only be detonated once they have been linked – or 'Chained' – into groups of at least three of the same colour. Multicoloured fireworks allow players to link many same-coloured firework Chains together to form 'Daisy Chains' that earn extra points and fill the screen with polychromatic particle effects when detonated. The single-player mode involves clearing a number of stages and replay value centres on creating ever-longer 'Daisy Chains'. The two-player simultaneous mode presents a split-screen with a dividing line that moves continuously according to performance, thereby increasing or reducing the play area available to each player. Victory comes when a player gains control of the entire play area – a device resurrected recently in *Lumines*.

Although derided in reviews and by players at launch as a dud, this is one time when it is OK to return to a firework that didn't go off first time.

Publisher: Sony Computer Entertainment Europe; **Platform**: Sony PlayStation 2.

Final Fantasy VII
1997
Square Co. Ltd

Currently sitting somewhere in the middle of one of the videogames industry's longest series, though moving inexorably towards the beginning of the cycle as yet more sequels are released, *Final Fantasy VII* is perhaps the best-known role-playing game (RPG). For Europeans at least, this will come as little surprise as for many years the genre was deemed too unpopular to warrant the release of even the best-selling and most critically acclaimed titles. Indeed, this seventh instalment was the first of the *Final Fantasy* series that European gamers were even given the chance to play. While this treatment might be irritating, or even galling, the consequences are not as severe as they could be. One could be forgiven for thinking that coming to a series part-way through would be a difficult and disorientating experience; like picking up a book half-way through or watching only the last part of a film trilogy. One might also reasonably assume that this problem would be compounded still further if it were known that complex narrative structures, rich character development and elaborate backstories were a central component of that videogame series. However, what is particularly interesting about the games of the *Final Fantasy* series is that while story, plot and character are, indeed, their defining qualities, the narratives are essentially self-contained.[11] This is no Homeric epic with a single tale broken into many chapters or even books; there is no central protagonist or hero whose journeys are our focus. Rather, each game presents a new storyline, with a set of new characters, twists, turns and denouements, though, perhaps confusingly, character names are frequently reused between games. Consequently, there is much change and difference across the twelve titles currently comprising the canon and although this might create excitement and anticipation in an audience, there is considerable opportunity for the developers to quickly and comprehensively alienate and even lose a fanbase.

As games, anybody familiar with *Dungeons & Dragons* will immediately recognise some of the basic mechanisms that underpin *Final*

Fantasy. In contrast to the real-time combat found in games such as Nintendo's *Legend of Zelda* series, Square's is a turn-based system in which players attack and defend in sequence, selecting actions from a menu-driven interface. As such, the games do not privilege speedy reactions or reflexes so much as thoughtful strategising and tactical manoeuvring. Furthermore, and owing a debt to board and tabletop role-playing games, players are required to develop their characters and build up their power and experience through victory in battle, while increasingly complex systems have been implemented to manage magical attacks, for example.

Final Fantasy VII's greatest contribution to the series also highlighted one of the most significant concerns. Being the first game to launch on PlayStation, and harnessing the fledgling CD-ROM technology, *Final Fantasy VII* made extensive use of full-motion video (FMV) sequences. That is, much of the extensive backstory and plot development was delivered through what amounted to movies – sequences that cannot be interacted with per se and over which the player, consequently, exercises no direct control. Like *Metal Gear Solid*, the balance between the FMV/playable sequences favours the former and leaves the player spending much time watching rather than doing, spectating rather than playing. Nonetheless, *Final Fantasy VII* is fondly remembered by players and, in its native Japan, readers of *Famitsu* magazine placed it second in their March 2006 list of all-time favourite games with only *Final Fantasy X* beating it to the top honour.[12]

11. The notable exception to this principle is *Final Fantasy X-2*, which develops the storyline of *Final Fantasy X* and follows the adventures of Yuna some two years on from the first game. Despite the narrative continuity of these two titles, their gameplay is quite different and like the rest of the *Final Fantasy* series, innovations and additional complexity mark out successive titles.

12. <www.next-gen.biz/index.php?option=com_content&task=view&id=2401&Itemid=2>.

Publisher: Sony Computer Entertainment Europe; **Platform**: PlayStation.

FreQuency
2001
Harmonix

Ultimately, *FreQuency* is a rhythm action game like *Dance Dance Revolution* or *Beatmania*, which presents music as a central tenet of its gameplay rather than as a backdrop or accompaniment to the action. However well integrated they might be, and however effective they might be in creating the atmosphere of the experience, the tunes in games such as *WipEout* or *Lumines* are essentially incidental to the act of piloting a spaceship at breakneck speed around a series of sinuous tracks, or arranging multicoloured blocks. In *FreQuency*, by contrast, the player's actions are entirely focused on the act of performing the tunes themselves. Indeed, *FreQuency*'s dedication to musical performance sets it apart even from many other rhythm action games. While in *PaRappa the Rapper*, for example, the object of the exercise is to rap along in time to a pre-recorded backing track in a manner not dissimilar to karaoke, in *FreQuency*, the musical track is built up almost in its entirety through the player's actions. In this way, *FreQuency* actually shares much in common with Nintendo's experimental 'playable media art' title *Electroplankton*, yet here there is none of that title's self-conscious innovation in interface design or the ways in which the production and performance of music is virtualised. In place of *Electroplankton*'s admittedly elegant touch screen controls and the whimsical conceit that sees subaquatic creatures emitting musical tones as they interact with one another and their environment, *FreQuency* takes the tools of the recording studio and replaces QWERTY and musical keyboards with the PlayStation's Dual Shock joypad. There is no doubt that *FreQuency* is a videogame, but it is not simply a videogame about music. It is not even a game that explores the ways in which music can be performed with a videogame interface as *Electroplankton* might be. Rather, *FreQuency* is a videogame about recording music with the kind of multitrack sequencing software that one would expect to find in a recording studio. As they zoom along an octagonal tube that extends 'into' the screen, the player is engaged in an experience akin to recording into a professional audio package such as Pro Tools, Cubase or Logic by playing the 1980s arcade game *Tempest*.

What distinguishes *FreQuency* from its generic rhythm action counterparts is that each tune is broken down into a number of constituent parts: drums, basslines, synthesiser and guitar riffs, pads and vocals; each need to be performed to build up the finished tune. There is no rapping over the top of a breakbeat here. The object of *FreQuency* is to gradually build up the full musical score one track at a time through a series of overdubs just as one would in a recording studio and the player is simultaneously the performer and producer of the game's tunes.

The gameplay revolves around two-bar looping sequences and demands that the player capture perfect performances of each instrument or musical part in turn before moving onto the next, usually more complex, two-bar sequence and repeating the process. Performing each instrumental part, whether percussive or pitched, is a matter of rhythm and the player must tap along on their joypad in time with a series of visual markers that appear on screen in order to play the notes and beats. On each facet of this octagon chute appear the bar lines and note hitpoints for each instrument and the player is literally surrounded by the music. Visually, then, the *Tempest*-inspired wireframe tube down which the player inexorably plummets not only evokes a retro-chic game aesthetic, but becomes a 3D representation of the music itself. Structurally, the chunking into two-bar sequences means that progress through the game is directly mapped to progress through the tune being played and this further adds to the sense in which this is a journey through the music itself.

Although they are quite different games, *FreQuency* owes something of a debt to *WipEout* in mining a similar aesthetic of techno dance music or electronica and making extensive use of licensed tracks from acts such as Orbital, Roni Size, Jungle Brothers and Paul Oakenfold. A sequel, *Amplitude*, was released in 2003. The game followed a similar pattern to its predecessor but added new musical tracks to perform.

Publisher: Sony Computer Entertainment Inc.; **Platform**: Sony PlayStation 2.

God of War
2005
Sony Computer Entertainment Studios Santa Monica

'This is to prove that games aren't just about dwarves and elves!' shouted a Rockstar representative upon receiving the Best Game award at GDC 2003 for *Grand Theft Auto III*. After Rockstar demonstrated that videogames are capable of being inhabited by more grown-up protagonists and dealing with issues with considerable contemporary cultural currency, the publishing fraternity clamoured to try and replicate their hard-edged street culture in other titles. The post-*Grand Theft Auto* marketplace saw publishers scrambling to exploit the hitherto relatively untapped area of 'mature' gaming. 'Mature content' thereafter became a shorthand for irony, violence and profanity. Concerned with supplying 'edge' and credibility, these games have displayed a decidedly immature attitude towards maturity. Curiously, for all its swearing, brutality and desolate urban wastelands, mature content in videogames has shied away from sex. You can almost hear the sniggering as the word is mentioned.

In the face of this recent history of mature gaming, *God of War* stands out as an anomaly. It has no 'urban' aspirations to satisfy, no authentic contemporary social dysfunction to capture and no hip licence to lean on. Having no pretensions to give the player a self-consciously 'adult' experience, the game is utterly bereft of the disconnected irony that runs through many contemporary mature titles. This game is wholly centred around the player and ensuring they receive the most spectacular, visceral experience possible. To play it is to palpably feel that a large team of people have invested a huge amount of effort and care into making you feel incredibly and intoxicatingly powerful.

Set in the world of ancient Greek mythology, the game pays detailed attention to its inspiration. The game draws as much upon the narrative conceits of this world as it does the expansive structural architectures and vicious cast of residents. The game hangs its narrative colours to the

God of War: and then it started raining

mast at the very opening of the game, as your character, Kratos, apparently commits suicide by throwing himself from Mount Olympus. The gameplay becomes the journey to this moment, an experience that is as exhilarating and as it is linear. Like the most successful narrative action-adventures of recent years (for example, *Half-Life 2* and *Max*

Payne) *God of War* feels like a game on rails, there is seldom much question of where Kratos should go next – yet this doesn't detract from the fun. The sensation is one of being propelled from one violent encounter to the next, totally at the whim of the game – yet still feeling in total control. The challenges in the game, the only pauses in this journey, are either spatial puzzles or, more usually, combat.

God of War is notable for many things, extraordinary art direction, pompous orchestral score, beautifully measured power-up and combat system. However, the feature for which most players will remember it is the extraordinary intensity and extremity of its violence. Had Sam Peckinpah ever made a videogame of *Clash of the Titans*, this would be the likely result. The game works hard for its 18 rating and it fully deserves it.

But, it would be reductive to describe the violence in *God of War* as simply 'explicit', as it displays an imagination and aesthetic treatment of the physical trauma experienced that hasn't been seen before. (Even in its cut scenes, the game excels in its production values.) Building on the tradition established in *Mortal Kombat* for elaborate kills, Kratos executes an alarming and joyous brutality in his fighting that leaves the player equally appalled and intoxicated. A simple control system allows even the clumsiest player to find themselves knee-deep in the dead. Artful, literate and bristling with intelligence, *God of War* is the first Grand Guignol videogame.

Publisher: Sony Computer Entertainment; **Platform**: Sony PlayStation 2.

Gran Turismo: The Real Driving Simulator
1998
Polyphony Digital

There has rarely been a shortage of driving games for any videogame console and the PlayStation has proved no exception, offering would-be racers numerous opportunities to burn virtual rubber. Sony's console launched with a virtually pixel-perfect conversion of Namco's *Ridge Racer* and has played host to sequels and updates of this series, as well as a host of games such as *Colin McRae Rally* and *Formula One* that cover ground as diverse as rally and F1 driving. To beat the congestion, any new racing game hoping to overtake the competition needs a unique selling point. Rather than enlist the services of a famous driver or focus on just one type of racing, *Gran Turismo* opted for realism. This may seem less than unique at first glance as one of the PlayStation's greatest strengths as a gaming device had been to allow developers to present increasingly realistic in-game graphics and players had soon become accustomed to exquisitely modelled and textured vehicles, tracks and scenery. However, the solidity of *Gran Turismo*'s cars, the way in which they rocked on their suspension as they sped through chicanes, and the way the specular reflections glinted on the cars' pristine bodywork, was a sight that few gamers were prepared for. In fact, the greatest problem was that all of this beauty was largely invisible to the player sitting 'inside' their shiny new supercar concentrating on the road ahead rather than the aesthetics of environment or machinery. So as not to let the hard work of the developers go to waste, and to enable the player to enjoy the spectacle of this slice of realism, *Gran Turismo* pioneered the action replay – complete the race and relax back into your armchair to watch yourself drifting round the corners. *Gran Turismo* allows you to be both driver and spectator at once. This is not simply a videogame about driving, this is a videogame about the television coverage of driving.

But it is also a videogame about the job of being a mechanic. *Gran Turismo*'s realism extends far further than its graphics or even the painstakingly recorded sounds that sample the engine notes of the real cars modelled in the game. Realism in *Gran Turismo* extends to tweaking and tuning almost every conceivable setting on the car from front–rear brake balance through to gear ratios and camber angles to wring those last few horsepower from the machine. This, as the subtitle proudly proclaims, is not merely a videogame about racing cars, this is *The Real Driving Simulator*, and while there is a 'Quick Arcade Mode' for those wanting the instant gratification of a supercar, it is in 'Gran Turismo Mode' that the title's relentless fixation with simulation and verisimilitude becomes apparent, even to the point where the player has to earn a racing licence before they can enter certain competitions. And for many, this obsession with simulation is the game's greatest problem. There is no doubt that this is a serious, perhaps even, dour experience and there is certainly none of the exuberance and histrionics found in *Outrun*, for example. The doughnuts and never-ending powerslides are replaced with a second-hand car garage where you pick up your first motor and try to earn enough credits from competition victories to either soup it up or trade it in for a nippier model. As the series has continued to develop, many critics have expressed concern that the almost maniacal devotion to simulation has squeezed out the fun from the experience of play.[13]

Paradoxically, for others it is the inconsistency of *Gran Turismo*'s simulation that is the game's weakness. Chief among the concerns is the lack of car damage. It is almost as though the game's 3D modellers are so proud of their virtual creations that they will not allow them to be tarnished in any way – even if the player crunches into a barrier or another car at top speed. And this is likely to happen as one of *Gran Turismo*'s other foibles is its physics models, frighteningly accurate in some senses, and yet allowing them to bounce off scenery and other cars with comparative impunity. The quickest way round a corner in *Gran Turismo* often takes advantage of the pinball-flipper qualities of a competitor's side panel. The real driving simulator or virtual bumper cars?

Whatever the criticisms, *GT* remains a critical franchise, not only for Sony but also for the manufacturers of the cars featured in the game.

Numerous promotional versions of the game exist dedicated to particular manufacturers or even models, and the game has been credited with raising the brand awareness of Japanese marques such as Subaru and models such as the Impreza and Nissan Skyline outside their native Japan. *Gran Turismo*: The Real Car Showroom Simulator.

13. See the review at <worldofstuart.excellentcontent.com/gt4/review-gt4.htm> for more on the clash between simulation and fun.

Publisher: Sony Computer Entertainment Europe; **Platform**: Sony PlayStation.

Grand Theft Auto: Vice City
2002
Rockstar North

No one *really* saw it coming. *GTA* had arrived on PlayStation and PC some years earlier and delivered its open-ended, mission-based, soundtrack-underscored brand of utterly amoral thrills to an audience that was enthusiastic but not by any means hysterical. The hallmarks of the series were established, but visually this was far removed from the *GTA* that was to become the infamous and internationally recognised franchise. The top-down, almost 2D representation nodded back to driving/cop games of the earlier era such as *Siren City* and *Spy Hunter*.

The huge environment itself is beautifully designed and seductive to explore – the game ships with a map to help players find their way around its labyrinthine backstreets. A first sequel kept the gameplay and visual design broadly the same, but moved the context to 1960s London. Players were reasonably indifferent to the changes.

It wasn't until 2001 that *Grand Theft Auto III* extruded the gameplay into a full 3D, third-person experience. Suddenly looking more like a modern-videogame archetype than a piece of kitsch retro, one might have expected *GTA III* to mark the point at which the franchise really exploded. This quantum shift in the presentation of the game was met with critical acclaim and sold well – but didn't ignite consumer frenzy.

GTA: Vice City subtly tweaked the gameplay, subtly improved the graphical performance – and relocated the action to a new place, new time and (crucially) new culture. Where *GTA III* was urban decay, *Vice City* was a sunny, pastel city by the sea – loosely modelled on Miami, Florida. The game was the first realisation of the full abilities of Rockstar North to neatly pastiche, paraphrase and reference entire pop-culture moments into neat packages of consumer videogame. *Vice City* gave the player an opportunity to inhabit a specific recollection of 1986 as filtered through American entertainment culture. Its reference points are witty, prescient and extraordinarily dense. It flew from the shelves and made eager gangsters of millions of gamers across the world.

Upon booting on the PC version, the game recreated the Commodore 64 loading screen and 'fastloader' coloured stripes. This knowing reference filled twenty-something gamers with a warm glow as hours of their childhoods were flashed before them. Before the game had even begun, we knew we were back in the early 1980s. The game goes on to deliver us a *Miami Vice* cityscape, utterly complete in every last reference from transport to pastel-suited fashion. Leaping down from the posters on the walls of student flats across the world, the influence of Brian De Palma's *Scarface* is particularly present. The game delivers us casual racism towards Cubans and Haitians (which was later removed following pressure from, among others, New York Mayor Michael Bloomberg), casual violence (including a blood-filled hotel room with a recently used chainsaw) and bountiful profanity. The game even places its finale battle inside an opulent mansion highly reminiscent of its film equivalent.

But Rockstar's understanding of the seductive power of pop culture extended well beyond simple visual and thematic quotation. An incredibly complex and dense set of cultural cues immerse the player in an efficient precis of an entire media landscape from their past. Developing the licensed soundtracks from the previous titles, *GTA: Vice City* pushed them further into the foreground, releasing an album of music from the game. Understanding the power of celebrity, the game uses the voiceover talents of actors such as Ray Liotta, Burt Reynolds, Dennis Hopper and *Miami Vice* star Phillip Michael Thomas. Understanding the power of restraint, the game features the voice of Debby Harry as a taxi-dispatcher.

Audaciously self-aware, *Vice City* stands alongside *WipEout* as a moment where a videogame confidently claimed a place in pop culture for itself. Few titles have achieved the kind of referential complexity of the title as successfully: a landmark moment for gaming and a portent of troubles yet to come. *GTA* has proved to be one of the causes célèbres of modern videogaming, provoking hysterical reaction from moral guardians and extraordinary demand from consumers. Perhaps a useful point of focus for discussion in the future might be not whether *GTA* actively devalues women or immigrant communities but rather what it does to *help*. Rockstar have yet to file a contribution to this discussion, although the 2005 'Hot Coffee' scandal in the sequel to *Vice City* indicates something about where their thinking lies.

Publisher: Rockstar Games; **Platform**: Sony PlayStation 2.

Guitar Hero
2005
Harmonix Music Systems

There is a long tradition of releasing bespoke controllers for specific videogame titles. Recent years have given us bongos, golf clubs and now – a '⅓ size Gibson SG replica'. Any glance you catch of yourself in a mirror while playing *Guitar Hero*, however, won't make you appear like you're holding an instrument of any such authenticity. Rather, and better, you're holding a plastic toy with brightly coloured fret-buttons and a white strum-bar. While you might be striking the poses of a rock star, the controller keeps you looking like a joyous child. It's almost impossible to resist the invitation to perform, not just play, as you face up to the fearsome challenge of 'Bark at the Moon'.

Unlike many of the music titles that have preceded it, *Guitar Hero* innovates by delivering something much more than a simple rhythm/response game such as *PaRappa the Rapper* or *Gitaroo Man*. *Guitar Hero* is more than a rhythm game, it's a music game. It's about pitch, rhythm and, most importantly, *performance*. Somehow, the sum of the controller device, coupled with the childishly simple play mechanic, wrapped around the self-aware pomposity of cock-rock classics by Queen, Boston *et al.* add up to a euphoric fictional rockumentary in which the player is the triumphant lead soloist. Not least through the choice of music and the particular kind of response it invokes in its listeners, the game forces participation not just as player but as performer in the band. The feeling is not one of rhythm/response, but of palpably playing music. Despite the gamely conceit of 'score' being present, the drive while playing it isn't to get a place at the high-score table, but to give the best performance.

The game is innately musical and commits wholly to the conceit that the player is in the band, playing their part of an arrangement. The challenge is not in learning some arbitrary set of motions in sync with a song, but in learning to play *your* part of the arrangement to the best of your ability. Developers Harmonix have invested in exploring and translating the musicality of the songs into fun, without ever simplifying their structures. There are phrases, verses, choruses, riffs, solos and, as to be expected within popular music, there is huge repetition. There is no shying away from having to solidly lay down your part of the song while the vocal is being delivered in this game. It's not just about being a guitar hero when the moment comes, it's about being in a band.

The game skilfully manages its varying levels of difficulty. While the complexity and skill of your performance is delivered remains the same, the game increases the complexity of your interactions with the frets to create the increasing challenge. In this way, even players on easy level can feel like they rock. The game partially shares a trait with a number of recent games such as *Prince of Persia* or *King Kong*, which, through a graceful animation triggered by a very simple user input, give the player the feeling of extraordinary skill. On its harder levels, however, *Guitar Hero* becomes a profoundly difficult challenge. Suddenly, you begin to understand that you need to practise in order to nail that solo and start to develop techniques for playing better, faster, with more precision. *Guitar Hero* teaches the player a lot about music, but it doesn't teach them how to play the guitar. Perhaps the greatest achievement of the game is to make you feel that you have genuinely learned to play a new instrument.

Publisher: Red Octane; **Platform**: Sony PlayStation 2.

Half-Life 2
2004
Valve

As few games have been as anticipated as this sequel to the paradigm-breaking *Half-Life*, few developers could have had the resources to expend on production as Valve did with this project. With the release of the original *Half-Life* in 1998, Valve (using a heavily modified *Quake* game engine) demonstrated the depth of narrative immersion that was possible within the basic model of a first-person shooter and won huge critical acclaim in doing so. Significantly, building on the culture of mod-making that had reached critical mass with *DOOM* and *Quake*, Valve shipped the final version of *Half-Life* complete with a copy of *Worldcraft*, the level design tool they used to model the game. In doing so they directly propagated the embedding of *Half-Life* culture into a growing web-based community of mod-makers. One of the mods, an anti-terrorist-themed game called *Counter Strike*, went on to become the most played online FPS of all time.

Half-Life 2, which was finally officially announced in 2003, became the subject of frenzied speculation and occasional controversy when the source code of the game was leaked onto the Internet. Originally slated for September of 2003, the game was dogged by delays before its final release in autumn 2004.

In both the extraordinary visual fidelity of the new 'source' engine constructed for the game, and the rigour with which the art direction was conceived, *Half-Life 2* demonstrates the way forward for the elusive 'interactive cinema' project more effectively than any other game before it. But it would be a disservice to suggest that the immersion the title manages to employ is wholly attributable to graphical excellence. Its predecessor, while far less graphically impressive, demonstrated the same skill for aping cinema. Valve are incredibly skilled magpies of cinematic genre systems and conventions, but it is their understanding that cinema and game shall ultimately never fuse that is their greatest asset.

The sensation of playing *Half-Life 2* is not that of playing a game. While there are game-like elements within it, particularly and most obviously in the combat sequences and physics-puzzle challenges, *Half-Life 2* is ultimately reaching towards something else. The feeling while playing is of being propelled at high velocity through a series of exciting events and utterly engaging atmospheres. The player is subtly guided down these paths by almost imperceptible cues to their own motivation. While City 17 feels (and indeed is) incredibly big, one is never lost within its streets because it is always clear which way the next goal lies. It is a game played almost on rails, but it feels completely free.

When the player becomes involved in action sequences, they are totally aware of their part within it as they have seen it rehearsed in decades of action movies. The stolen glances and audible footsteps of stealthy assassins from Bruce Lee, the precarious balancing while under gunfire of James Bond and the diving underwater for cover from the fire of an explosion from countless Hollywood action movies. Valve skilfully quote entire sequences from a wide variety of reference points to deliver the player to a world they wholly understand. The player has simply been there before. But rather than subtract from the pleasure, this is the greatest driver of it.

Valve were also careful, however, to deliver a complex and satisfying narrative. In the intelligent scripting of Marc Laidlaw, *Half-Life 2* telegraphs a dense story of oppression and conspiracy – importantly, all through the first-person viewpoint. The game again refuses to break from this sole window into the action, an interesting shift from the popular model of using 'cut scenes' for story exposition. The narrative still plays out in scripted conversations in front of the player but the player can receive the story from wherever they choose to stand; essentially passive moments of exposition but still feeling wholly participative and engaging. The talking figures in front of them frequently address the player directly, implicating them directly in the action – reinforcing their immersion and involvement in the narrative. It is in the design of the 'lead' and the player protagonist, Gordon Freeman, where Valve maintain the masterstroke played in the original game. Gordon never speaks. In this simple device of silence, Valve instil more agency for the player in the fictional videogame world than any number of branching narrative lines can provide.

Publisher: Valve; **Platform**: PC.

Hapland
2005
Robin Allen

The frustrations of the point-and-click adventure game seem to have been internalised by designer Robin Allen. Most evident in titles like *Myst*, the sensation of wiping the screen with the cursor until it becomes a 'hand' and signifies some potential interaction has given millions of gamers millions of hours of frustration. *Hapland*, his extraordinary puzzle landscapes, takes that frustration and exaggerates it way beyond all reasonable design. The original game, released in early 2005, was an acclaimed hit in the casual game scene and Allen has since created two more sequels. It's cruelly unforgiving, frequently requires you to reset the game because you're stuck in a dead end and follows a puzzle logic that is consistent to itself, but bewildering to most outsiders. Almost inexplicably, it's incredibly addictive.

Hapland hinges on the player's willingness to reiterate. It's a persistent cycle of rehearsing and re-rehearsing cause and effect until a sequence begins to form. The game relies heavily on player addiction, particularly on their patience with the repetitive trial-and-error play escalating into an obsessive grudge. To offset this, the visual design of *Hapland* is disarmingly simple, a gently surreal style that cunningly masks the cruel gameplay. The detailed landscape is lovingly drawn from pastel hues and serves to calm you during the more unreasonably frustrating puzzles.

Perversely for a so-called 'casual' game, *Hapland* is anything but. It requires, in fact, in its own stubborn way, *demands*, that you give it your entire attention. After doing so it rewards you with little more than the whimsy of the designer. It's a huge compliment to the balancing act it walks that you feel like forgiving, and then congratulating, Allen for his ridiculous, tortuous logic.

Publisher: Foon; **Platform**: Browser-Based Flash.

Harvest Moon
1997
Natsume

For detractors of videogames, and there are many, *Harvest Moon* is a real problem. If games are all about shooting, kicking and reinforcing violence and aggression as strategies for success, then what should one make of a game where the object is to bring in a bumper crop of turnips and develop an affectionate relationship with your cows so that they yield more milk?

Harvest Moon is an unusual game. Most obviously, it is one of that rare breed of farming simulators (Maxis' *Sim Farm* being a notable counterpart ploughing this comparatively lonely furrow) in which guns and lasers are replaced by hoes and pitchforks, mindless violence is supplanted by

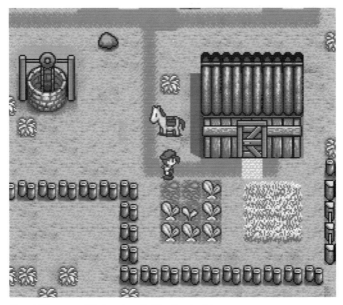

Harvest Moon: one of that rare breed of farming simulators

thoughtful nurturing, and the gritty realism of post-apocalyptic urban decay blossoms into tranquil, rural idyll. Originally released in 1997 for the SNES and followed by many sequels, *Harvest Moon* puts the player in the role of a young man bequeathed a farm by his grandmother and charges them with the task of turning this dilapidated homestead into a profitable concern by raising livestock and growing crops that can be sold, so effectively integrating the farmstead into the local economy. In this way, *Harvest Moon* is an, albeit simplistic, business simulator that presents players with choices such as whether to lay a field to grass to make hay for animal feed, or whether to sell eggs or incubate them to hatch more chickens. And these choices have real consequences. People's (and animals') lives are at stake here.

But there's no urgency. Important though they may be, these decisions cannot be rushed. Crops don't just grow overnight. And this is another of *Harvest Moon*'s notable features. The pacing and tempo of the game so perfectly evoke the passing of the seasons that the player soon tunes into the rhythms of the earth, becoming sensitive to its needs and demands and working in harmony with the game's nature to reap rewards.

But *Harvest Moon* is not only about crops and microeconomics. It is also concerned with cultivating relationships. After dark, villagers gather at the bar to gossip and, over time, the player may catch the eye of one of the girls in town, perhaps even getting married and having children. And herein lies one of *Harvest Moon*'s problems. While its approach to game design may be novel, even revolutionary, in its steadfast refusal to follow the pack, its take on gender politics is rather less than enlightened. You are a man, and you must marry to progress through the game. The release of *Harvest Moon for Girl* may be seen as a concession or as exacerbating the problem.

It is easy to dismiss *Harvest Moon* as a piece of nostalgia – as a sepia-tinged slice of bucolic hyperreality – but it is more than just a peculiarity. Because in so many ways it is the antithesis of what videogames have become it exists both as a respite from their insistence and spectacle, and a commentary on them.

Publisher: Natsume; **Platform**: Super Nintendo Entertainment System.

The Hobbit
1982
Beam Software

The text-adventure genre was at its height in the early to mid-1980s. From their beginnings as text-only works, frequently taking place in the locale of caves – many of which had mazes – they had developed rapidly into a varied form. In particular, the work of Brian Howarth and his 'Mysterious Adventure' titles and the phenomenal output of Scott Adams drove the games and the narrative worlds they explored further into the mainstream gamer audience. Adams in particular, in a long-standing relationship with Marvel Comics, demonstrated the potential richness of a licensed product.

While it might be difficult today to imagine a time when the world of Tolkien wasn't a closely controlled media franchise, in 1983 things were very different. *The Hobbit*, programmed by Australian studio Beam Software (who would go on to create seminal C64 beat-em-up *Way of the Exploding Fist*), was a critically acclaimed title, which was usually supplied with a copy of the book when sold.

While 'You are about to play the most sophisticated game program yet devised for any microcomputer' might seem like a lofty claim – it was not without some basis in fact. *The Hobbit* introduced a number of key innovations to the text-adventure form that significantly raised the bar for titles that followed. Aware that the innovations it was making were of some importance, publisher Melbourne House took the measures of registering a number of trademarks around them; thus Inglish, Animaction and Animtalk were born.

Inglish was the most immediately conspicuous. For the first time, the input parser used to play the game had been extended from the hitherto limiting two words (go west, open door, kill troll, etc.). Inglish gifted the player with the ability to enter complete sentences to guide Bilbo through his quest; indeed the manual boasted that the program was even able to recognise multiple sentences at once (although it did concede that there is a total limit of 128 characters in any one input)!

The game also made strides towards the establishment of some degree of autonomy for the non-player characters that inhabited the world. The game was played in 'real-time', if the player didn't enter any text for thirty seconds the game would report that 'time-passes'; and while it was doing so, every other character was busy going about their business. This innovation served to create an environment that truly felt alive with possibility. Coupled with the 'Animtalk' mechanism for addressing individual characters, the player began to feel like they were in a truly free world.

It's in the tension between this illusion of total freedom and the need for the game to deliver the narrative experience of *The Hobbit*, as all readers of the source text understand it, that the game is, in many ways, most fascinating. While contemporary developers struggle with ever more responsive and complex AI, *The Hobbit* delivered its illusion of reality through concentrating on a small series of hitherto unseen devices. The inclusion of a text-driven physics model was particularly persuasive, as the player was given the ability to place objects inside others, tether things together and prevented from being able to lift things that were too heavy. Within a fantastical world, the developers concentrated on delivering the environmental basics that made it believable. With time, gravity, character and physics all made tangible, the wizards, orcs and dragons could concentrate on being fantastic.

Publisher: Melbourne House; **Platform**: ZX Spectrum, Commodore 64, BBC Micro, Dragon 32, MSX, Oric, Apple II, PC.

Ico
2002
Sony Computer Entertainment Inc.

'Subtlety' and 'delicacy' might not be two words commonly associated with videogames and yet they perfectly sum up *Ico*. In many ways, *Ico* is the antithesis of videogames and certainly challenges almost every preconception that one might have about them both in terms of form and aesthetics. Where some videogames are loud and brash, *Ico* is quiet and contemplative. Where some videogames attempt to burst the player's eardrums with blaring music and sound effects, *Ico*'s soundscape is comprised almost exclusively of environmental effects with only the barest of musical themes played at a few moments throughout the game. The screen is similarly sparse with none of the usual health meters and other iconography. Where some videogames assault the eyes with explosions that fill the screen and arm the player with an arsenal of guns, lasers, grenades and other weaponry, *Ico* places in your hand a plank of wood with which to fend off evil. *Ico* is no ordinary videogame. Indeed, so great are the differences that creator Fumito Ueda prefers not to call it a game at all.[14]

The plot is simple enough. You are Ico, a young boy born in a small village. However, you are born with horns protruding from your head. Every ill that befalls the village is blamed on you and, on your twelfth birthday, you are taken from the village to a distant, ruined building and left for dead so as to banish your curse once and for all. Though the villagers believe the building to be deserted, upon waking from your slumber and exploring this prison, you stumble across a wisp-like girl trapped in a cage hanging from the ceiling. Her name is Yorda, and together you form an alliance that sees you attempting to find a path back to your world. While the two characters are equally foregrounded, you control only Ico in the game. Yorda is no shrinking damsel in distress in need of rescue, though, and she offers help and assistance throughout the game and you soon realise that the characters are essentially inseparable. Indeed, for the most part, Ico and Yorda hold hands – as much, it seems, for emotional support as pathfinding or guidance. Leaving Yorda alone for too long sees ghostly, wisp-like, spirits appear and attempt to drag her into a black, swirling chasm that opens up in the ground. The effect is genuinely chilling, partly because of the sumptuous and understated animation and partly because of the strength of the emotional bond between you and the young girl.

Ico's world is one of extraordinary scale. The great castle towers above Ico and Yorda, views stretch to the horizon and ravines plunge into darkness below. In some senses, this is a forbidding world. This was, after all, to be your last resting place and its labyrinths and traps are as much, if not more, a part of the challenge as the spirits that seek out Yorda. And yet, the environment is rendered with such extraordinary detail that the feeling is one of awe. The hazy light and desaturated tones lend an ethereal, dreamlike, other-worldly quality, the vertiginous camera angles accentuate the scale of the architecture and natural surroundings, making you feel small and abandoned, and all the while Yorda offers kinship and support, and yet you are reminded that you are both utterly dependent upon, and responsible for, her. The faint whistle of the wind in the trees and the hollow echoing of your own footsteps heighten your senses of perception, making you more aware of your environment, its beauty, and the fact that the fate of you and Yorda is inextricably bound to it. Though from the outset it is clear that this is a world that you are lost within and that not only dwarfs you but that can literally swallow you up, it soon becomes clear that the only way to secure your escape is to work with it rather than against it. Unlike some videogames where your objective is to fight through hordes of enemies while making incidental progress through a world, here the world itself is the puzzle and solution.

Fans of *Ico* have long clamoured for further instalments and have been keen to view 2005's *Shadow of the Colossus* as a sequel. However, though official marketing materials have been quite meticulous in avoiding any mention of *Ico*, numerous teasers and hints dotted throughout *Shadow* have led a number of fans to suggest that it is, in fact, a prequel to *Ico*.

14. See the interview at Eurogamer for more on Ueda's vision for *Ico*:
   <www.eurogamer.net/article.php?article_id=63179>.

Publisher: Sony Computer Entertainment Europe; **Platform**: Sony PlayStation 2.

Ikaruga
2001 (Coin-Op); 2002 (Dreamcast and GameCube)
Treasure

It is almost impossible to discuss Treasure's *Ikaruga* without at least some
mention of the company's earlier arcade and Sega Saturn game *Radiant
Silvergun*. Both games are vertically scrolling shoot-em-ups, both are
ruthlessly difficult, and while neither achieved great commercial success,
both are fêted by fans and reviewers. Although Treasure have never
officially named *Ikaruga* as the sequel to *Radiant Silvergun*, tantalising
indicators, including a reference to 'Project RS2', are buried in the game's
text. As such, the game is understood as the 'spiritual successor' if not a
true sequel[15] and there are certainly many similarities. The emphasis,
considered and planned destruction, remains at the heart of the game
and indiscriminate blasting is as unrewarded here as before. Chaining the
destruction of like-coloured enemies into lengthy – sometimes whole
stage-long – sequences is again the order of the day and, as attack
patterns in *Ikaruga* are pre-ordained, it is possible if not essential to
memorise and strategise.

For all these apparent similarities, however, *Ikaruga* is a very different
game. The seven-weapon system is replaced by a seemingly paltry single
laser (with the capacity to charge and unleash a more powerful shot).
More significantly, though, where *Radiant Silvergun* is a riotous, opulent
explosion of colour that draws from a wide palette and paints its ships in
bold colours, *Ikaruga*'s is an understated and decidedly monochromatic
aesthetic. Gone is the three-colour variation of enemy craft and in its
place comes a system of 'polarity'. Everything in *Ikaruga* is black or
white, and although that might conjure up ideas of simplicity, it is
actually the root of the game's extraordinary complexity. Polarity is
explored and embedded into the gameplay in an even more fundamental
manner than in *Radiant Silvergun*, where colour variation facilitated
chaining and the attainment of high scores. In *Ikaruga*, the polarity of
each enemy craft, and every bullet they fire, is significant not merely

because of the desire to chain hits together for points bonuses, but because the player's ship reacts differently to black or white enemies, because it is also subject to polarity. With the flick of a controller button, the player can switch the colour of their ship from black to white, not because they want to keep the screen tidy, but because the black bullets of black enemy ships cannot damage the player's ship if it is black. In fact, bullets of the same colour can be harvested for additional power (this technique is known as 'dot-eating' among *Ikaruga* players in a homage to *Pac-Man*). The trade-off, unfortunately, is that when the player's ship is the same polarity as an enemy craft, its weapons are only half as effective as if their polarities differed. And so, from this remarkably simple mechanic of black vs white comes a gameplay implementation of staggering intricacy and depth.

Ikaruga's difficulty level, its repeatable, predictable attack patterns and structure, and its perfectibility, have made it an ideal candidate for practitioners of 'super-play'. The object of super-play is to perform the game in the most complete manner by, for example, creating the longest chains of hits; or even in the most audacious manner, by tackling the simultaneous two-player mode single-handedly, taking both joysticks and controlling both ships at once, alone.[16] Watching *Ikaruga* super-play reveals an exceptional beauty in the performances not simply because these expert players embellish their manoeuvres with gratuitous flourishes, but because the refined structure and aesthetic of the game actively demands poise and grace. As play routines, attacks and routes are necessarily memorised and honed, there is a choreographed, almost balletic, quality to the performances (albeit a ballet in which almost everything gets destroyed by laser fire). While super-play occurs with other games,[17] it usually exists on the periphery of gaming culture and is indulged in by resolutely 'hardcore' players rather than the mainstream or 'ordinary' player. However, with *Ikaruga*, Treasure sought to normalise and integrate this most hardcore of gaming practice into the very fabric of the game. Practice modes that demonstrate perfect performances and allow players to attempt to replicate them at half the normal game speed encourage repeat play and refinement of technique by illustrating the difficulty of the stages and, by implication, the poverty of the player's current efforts. To hammer home the complexity and intensity of the game yet further, Treasure even released a DVD *Ikaruga Appreciate* with video footage of super-play performances along with notes and commentaries. Ultimately, *Ikaruga* is interesting in presenting a deeply challenging, intricate game that is based around an almost embarrassingly simple underlying gameplay concept of 'polarity' rather than technological gimmickry. After all, it does not even require a colour television.

15. <www.classicgaming.com/shmups/reviews/ikaruga/index.html>.
16. See <www.ikaruga.co.uk> for examples, discussion and video of super-play performances.
17. See <speeddemosarchive.com> for video clips of videogame super-play and speedruns.

Publisher: Sega (Dreamcast version), Atari (GameCube version); **Platform**: Coin-Op, Sega Dreamcast, Nintendo GameCube.

Impossible Mission
1983
Epyx

Of the many gifts the Commodore 64 SID chip bestowed upon gamers, the speech synthesis has not fared well with the passage of time. From triggering a cry of 'Ghostbusters!', in time to the music, to the martial arts scream of the *Way of the Exploding Fist* loading screen, it could be argued that it's difficult to see the function in these flourishes beyond that of a technology demo. But that would be to ignore the true genius of the smart use of this device, the establishment – through repetition, and then through nostalgia – of a catchphrase. In 1983, Epyx introduced a particularly enduring phrase to gamers when, upon beginning to play a game of *Impossible Mission*, they were greeted with the cry of an evil genius. 'Another visitor? Stay a while . . . Stay Forever!'

Trapped inside the complex underground lair of Professor Elvin Atombender, perhaps the first thing the player notices is how immaculately well animated they are. The game features a beautifully animated central character, who is both meticulously constructed in his sprints and somersault leaps – and utterly devoid of any character. While Atombender is given full licence to emote with the powers of primitive speech, the player is reduced to a token in a puzzle (excepting when he falls to his death – when he is granted a blood-curdling scream). *Impossible Mission* challenges the player to discover the thirty-six digits of the code, which will disarm the missiles Atombender has armed. However, these are hidden in random items of furniture that all have to be individually searched. The highly repetitive gameplay consists of running, searching and avoiding the foes that lie in your way. In a direct nod to the TV show *The Prisoner*, one of these enemies is an alarmingly speedy white ball.

What could easily become a dull game is saved through a series of clever design devices. None of the searchable items yield their secrets instantly – frequently the player is challenged with searching a little, jumping to avoid a robot, and then returning to continue the search later. This simple time demand produces an element of tension that carries the game through its thirty-two rooms of gameplay. In addition, with each play the game randomises the locations of each clue, thereby ensuring that even though the game itself might be broadly repetitious, it is never wholly predictable.

It was succeeded by a sequel in 1998 and was one of the key releases from the American developer Epyx, who produced a string of highly successful titles for the Commodore 64 in the early 1980s. Acclaimed for their high production values, these games included *Summer Games*, *Winter Games* and *Pitstop II,* among others.

Publisher: Epyx; **Platform**: Commodore 64.

J. D. Spy
2001
Michael Jacobs

Much like *Sphere of Chaos*, *J. D. Spy* is a wonderfully invigorating example of game design unconstrained by the tastes of publishers, focus groups or indeed any particular commercial imperative. Released for PC only in 2001 the game is acutely aware of the platform that it is built for, indeed it is a shining example of operating system-specific game design. Ironically, this isn't because of the skilful way in which the game leverages the capabilities of Windows to produce particularly brilliant graphical effects. Rather in its first, opening stages, the game skilfully refers to a commonly experienced system malfunction to declare its uniquely ambiguous boundaries of play.

Upon execution, the *J. D. Spy* 'software' conspicuously fails – a system error window flashing up alerting you to a debug process and confronting the player with lines of (apparently) indecipherable code. The scenario that the program has crashed is so accurately reproduced that many players simply stop at this point. It is the patient and inquisitive player who is prompted into investigating those lines of 'code' further, which slowly reveal directions explaining how to proceed. This audacious opening puzzle is a portent of what is to follow. *J. D. Spy* is a staggeringly unforgiving game.

Upon cracking this initial puzzle, the player is inducted into a world of espionage and intrigue. The 'game' environment itself has the appearance of a personal information manager, the sort that most players would already have installed on their personal computers. It is through the skilful maintenance of this relationship between the gameworld and the external world that *J. D. Spy* experiments with a number of radical ideas, many of which would find their commercial exploitation in titles such as *Majestic*, some time later. The specific conceit of software application as self-conscious game environment has also been successfully mined in the 1980s by Activision's *Hacker* and more recently by Introversion's *Uplink*.

J. D. Spy develops to present the player with a series of extraordinarily difficult puzzle scenarios, which require them variously to conducts web searches, 'log-on' to external machines using replicas of telnet clients and, perhaps most audaciously, require them to learn a little Java programming in order to proceed.

The game makes rigorous demands upon the player; indeed if ever there were a game that needed the player to 'want to believe' then this is it. Requiring a huge leap on the behalf of the player to indulge its delicate fiction, *J. D Spy* will undoubtedly not suit many tastes.

In the final assessment, the game is not so much 'difficult' as frustratingly obtuse. There are few players who would be able to intuit the solutions to all of *J. D. Spy* without resorting to an online walkthrough. Ironically, however, even then the project still yields enormous pleasure in the revelation of the sheer preposterousness of some of the problems. Spectacularly independent and wonderfully flawed.

Publisher: independent; **Platform**: PC.

Jet Set Willy
1984
Software Projects

One of defining titles of the 8-bit era, Matthew Smith's first game, *Manic Miner*, provided early home computer gaming with one of the closest things it had to an iconic hero. Miner Willy, the hero of the title, was to appear in another four 'official' sequels – before reaching immortality in an ongoing series of remakes, adapations and wholly original works featuring his durable likeness.

Manic Miner arrived onto the ZX Spectrum in 1983 and brought with it the first instance of in-game music (cunningly using only out-of-copyright classical tracks) and a particularly English sensibility. Its extraordinary success pushed the genre of the 'platform game' to the forefront of gaming and paved the way for the first and best-loved sequel.

Jet Set Willy took the essence of the art style and play mechanics of the original game and transferred it into an explorative format. Whereas the original game was constructed as a series of levels to be solved in sequence, *Jet Set Willy* placed the protagonist in a mansion constructed of (as the cassette inlay boasts) 'over 60 rooms'. The sense of scale that the game generates is extraordinary. Wandering around the huge mansion house map it is difficult not to be impressed at the sheer size of the undertaking. In 1984, a gameworld of this scale, in a game of this type, was simply unprecedented.

Like *Manic Miner*, *Jet Set Willy* provides a particularly unforgiving play experience. In an age before save-games were commonplace, the Miner Willy games set players an extraordinarily difficult task. The platform puzzles that form the anatomy of the game often relied on jumps being made at very specific (and thus very difficult) moments. More challenging than this, they frequently would demand the player be at a single specific point on a ledge in order to be able to complete the leap safely. This 'pixel-perfect' model of action gaming would stay with the genre for some years, the influence extending as far as the early games of the *Tomb Raider* series. Perhaps the greatest challenge of the original release of *JSW* was the fact that it was, in fact, impossible to complete – although fixes for this soon emerged.

The Miner Willy games, *JSW* in particular, elevated programmer Matthew Smith to the level of game-maker superstar. In the UK of the early 1980s, within the microcosm of computer games, there were few who achieved this status. The attention and money that this success brought Smith were to be short-lived however. He disappeared from public view for over a decade, igniting a global search (on the Internet at least) for his whereabouts and becoming an almost genuine enigma in the process. He was to reappear in Amsterdam some years later, slightly stoned and confused about the fuss.

One of the most interesting and perhaps unexpected legacies of the series has been the sheer volume of remakes and adaptations it has inspired. The original Spectrum game stored the source code for the levels entirely separately to the game code, allowing hackers to create their own levels relatively easily – in one of the first examples of modding of commercial videogames. The Internet yields vast archives of current Willy games in development. While maintaining the visual style of the original (coded for the ZX Spectrum and run under emulation) they display no shortage of ambition in the narratives they attempt to portray. Projects include, *Jet Set Willy: The Chronicles of Narnia*, *Jet Set Willy: The Lord of the Rings*; and perhaps most surprisingly, *Manic Miner: The Buddha of Suburbia*.

Publisher: Software Projects; **Platform**: ZX Spectrum.

Katamari Damacy
2004
Namco

Katamari Damacy has been lauded by fans and critics alike. The game has won countless awards and has won plaudits for its innovation and design. For maverick developer Keita Takahashi, however, it is important not to lose sight of the goal. 'I'm very honored that *Katamari Damacy* received various awards, and that it was called "innovative," but the most important thing is that people can laugh and enjoy themselves' (Leone, 2005). While this may be the stated aim of many videogame developers, *Katamari Damacy*'s extraordinary commitment to silliness ensures that a smile is never far away from the player's face. From the dancing pandas in the opening sequence to the ludicrous non sequiturs of the dialogue that introduces each level, *Katamari Damacy* is a game that leaves the player beaming. It is rare that a videogame is so utterly positive in its outlook. Takahashi's creation is a world of unbridled pleasure in which cynicism, pessimism and anger are wholly absent.

Although it is based around an extremely simple concept, *Katamari Damacy* defies explanation. The game falls into no existing genre, although it draws on many activities commonly found in videogames, such as exploration and collection. The premise sounds rather grand. In the role of the 5cm-high Prince of All Cosmos, the player's task is to replace the stars in the heaven that have been destroyed by their father, the King of All Cosmos. Depending on which territory the player purchases the game, the reason for this cosmic calamity varies. In the original Japanese release, it is the King's drunken antics that extinguish the starlight from the sky. This wanton excess did not sit well with the American publishers of the game, however, and in the sanitised US release, the King simply wakes up unable to remember what happened the night before. The tiny Prince is charged with the duty of replacing the stars before their absence is noted. To effect the subterfuge, the Prince is equipped with a 'katamari', a sticky ball to which objects adhere. Pushing the ball around the landscape, the player picks up increasingly large objects and grows the katamari to its target size. As the ball's diameter increases, so can successively more voluminous objects be rolled up, until the ball is sufficiently large that it can be jettisoned into space where it will, hopefully, be mistaken for one of the missing stars.

At its heart, *Katamari Damacy* is a game that might seem to involve nothing more exciting than rolling a sphere around a series of environments collecting objects and scenery in order to create as big a ball of garbage as possible. In practice, however, *Katamari Damacy* is a superbly executed piece of daftness that combines excellent character design with magnificent controls, and that plays with scale in the most imaginative way. Starting off in environments such as the interior of a house and rolling up an assortment of objects no larger than map pins and pencil erasers, the action soon shifts out of doors and animals, pedestrians and even cars soon get mixed up in the sticky katamari. Visual design assists greatly in establishing the game's considerable charm and highly stylised, deliberately crudely drawn and animated figures, arms and legs frantically flailing, are soon seen sticking out of the player's growing katamari. Towards the end of the game, cars, buildings, ships, whales and even whole islands can be rolled up and the very world in which the game takes place collapses into the singularity of the katamari, literally consumed by the Prince's rolling. Yet, for all these successes, the King of All Cosmos is never happy and continues to communicate the disappointment he feels for his son in the most amusingly impatient, strangely endearing and unique manner.

While the comparatively minimal dialogue is conveyed textually throughout the game, music and sound effects play an important role. Objects, whether animate or inanimate, make a characteristic noise as they are rolled into the katamari and whether it is the ring of a phone or the miaow of a cat, this auditory cue sends the corners of the player's mouth curling. The game's soundtrack is as eclectic and varied as the contents of a katamari ball with a wide array of genres ranging from glitchy techno workouts to breezy J-pop songs.

Katamari Damacy's style extends throughout the game and beyond into the game's packaging and even the official website. Where such 'support' materials and resources would usually bear some of the visual identifiers of the game and would be in keeping with the overall look and feel of the title, *Katamari Damacy*'s boxart, manual and website are not only entirely consistent but also develop the artistic direction of the game. The Flash games and desktop pictures available at <www.katamaridamacy.jp> are not, in themselves, revolutionary and certainly similar materials are available on countless other official game websites, but here they feel less like marketing and promotional fodder intended to extend the brand and more like an integral part of the game's aesthetic. Again, as with the soundtrack, diversity and variety are the watchwords and the mixed-up collection of different visual styles that comprise the downloadable wallpaper collection, for example, perfectly captures the jumble of the katamari itself.

Because it was deemed to have too limited an appeal, *Katamari Damacy* was never released in Europe although, curiously, its sequel, *We ♥ Katamari,* was rolled up and published in Europe by Electronic Arts in 2006. This title leaves much of the gameplay unaltered though adds a postmodern storyline that centres on the adoration of the fans that the diminutive Prince has acquired since his performance in the first game. A further sequel, *Me and My Katamari,* is to be released for Sony PSP in 2006. Whether *Katamari Damacy* heralds a new genre of 'roll-em-ups' remains to be seen, though Takahashi has indicated on many occasions that he wishes to pursue other avenues, not necessarily limited to videogames. Those who attended the Game Developers Conference Europe at which his impromptu design for a '. . . wifi-enabled, AI-enhanced, heated toy cat which could be used to manipulate house-bound grannies into a kind of competitive soup-making . . .'[18] was unleashed onto an unsuspecting audience who will have learned to expect the unexpected.

18. See *EDGE* magazine's feature, 'Everybody Loves Takahashi'. Available at <www.edge-online.co.uk/archives/2006/01/everybody_loves_1.php>.

Publisher: Namco; **Platform**: Sony PlayStation 2.

Killer 7
2005
Grasshopper Studios

This is for grown-ups. One of the most highly anticipated titles for the GameCube, the trailers for this title that hit the Internet appeared to show us a first-person shooter unlike anything we had seen before. While clearly riding the (then) vogue for cel-shaded graphics as exemplified by titles like *XIII* and *The Legend of Zelda: The Wind Waker*, this appeared to offer something very different and very adult. Appearing like a strange hybrid of *Reservoir Dogs*, *Tetsuo* and any Hong Kong John Woo movie, it thrust a striking visual world forward. Enemies when shot, paused, turned red, and then exploded into a million droplets of blood. They screamed at the player as abstract ribbons of blood spewed forth from their faces. It appeared that GameCube's reputation as the 'family console' might be under threat. Under the production guidance of Shinji Mikami, who created *Resident Evil*, *Devil May Cry* and *Viewtiful Joe* – players were expecting something different. In this respect at least, they weren't disappointed. It's probably fair to comment, however, that they weren't expecting something *this* different.

While clearly remarkable in its visual design, a short amount of time with the game reveals that the unique visual style is only the beginning of its eccentricities. The plot itself is a highly complex assassination story, in which the player takes the part of all seven assassins, moving between them as they choose. All sharing the surname 'Smith', the killer seven are all manifestations of the personality of a wheelchair-bound, sixty-year-old Harman Smith. (Incidentally, the game acknowledges the namesake Manchester miserablist band with the legend 'How Soon is Now?' scrawled on a wall during an early mission.) The use of the different characters and their individual abilities is key to progressing through the game, although few of them actually have their character exposited in any depth.

Perhaps the most contentious mechanic in the game is the means by which the player moves through the world. While looking visually like a

Killer 7: ribbons of blood spewed forth from their faces

third-person action game (albeit a heavily stylised one) it behaves anything but. Where a player might expect to be able to move freely through the 3D space, as in *GTA*, in fact the characters are all placed on rails. Moving the direction stick has no effect, the only control the player has is to move forward along a predetermined path, or turn around and come back. At junction points, options are presented for selection that are chosen directionally. This creates a strange and unusual experience, the sensation is of moving along the paths of a map and passing through explicitly declared nodes of choice – more like bivalent hypertext than playful freedom. Indeed, whereas other 3D worlds take great pains to give the impression of freedom, *Killer 7* effectively creates a formal claustrophobia.

There are combat sections, there are puzzles – but yet it doesn't feel like a game. It's something different. For its problems and inaccessibility, *Killer 7* provides a remarkable and unique sensory experience.

Publisher: Capcom; **Platform**: Nintendo GameCube, Sony PlayStation 2.

The Last Ninja
1987
System 3

Claimed by its makers to be the best-selling game on the Commodore 64 of all time, *The Last Ninja* is notable for the sheer epic scale of its ambitions – and the fact that it delivered on them on such a limited system. More than any game to that point, *The Last Ninja* took great pains to concentrate on atmosphere, which seduced and captured players who simply hadn't seen anything that *theatrical* on a C64 before. *The Last Ninja* had a po-faced pomposity about it that was intoxicating. As a complete package, it was so very, very serious about Ninja-ness that it was impossible not to believe in.

At heart it was a straight action-adventure game, built around prolonged periods of exploration punctuated with bouts of combat. The exploration itself was limited to the pathways on the terrain, but even within this constraint the sense was still of being part of a living world. Great investment had been made in the art design, dressing the terrains and interiors with detail that, while it couldn't be touched, felt like it had a meaningful purpose in the context of the game.

The game itself was incredibly difficult. In particular, the puzzles, which relied on micro-manoeuvres to make a jump from exactly the right position, proved hugely frustrating, although one might argue that Ninjas are supposed to be reasonably precise. Combat was equally tricky, with the eight degrees of movement afforded the player demanding a level of skill and precision they hadn't encountered before. Not in that many directions anyway. Previous martial arts combat games such as *Way of the Exploding Fist* only demanded a 2D approach.

Perhaps the most memorable facet of the game, though, is the exquisite soundtrack composed by Ben Daglish and Anthony Lees. Eleven full-length compositions were featured in the game, which were responsible in no small part for the overall atmosphere of the piece. The piece stands as a highlight of the SID chip's huge portfolio.

The first sequel, *Last Ninja 2: Back with a Vengeance*, was also very well received – acclaimed by many as being an improvement on the original. *Last Ninja 3: Real Hatred is Timeless* was less well received.

Publisher: System 3; **Platform**: Commodore 64.

The Legend of Zelda: Ocarina of Time
1998
Nintendo EAD

Few videogames have been so universally lauded as Shigeru Miyamoto's fifth *The Legend of Zelda* (*LoZ*) instalment. Reflecting its rapturous reception and near unanimous perfect scores, the game currently sits at the top of the Metacritic[19] and Gamerankings[20] databases of videogames reviews and it ranks as the first game (and still one of only six) ever to have received a perfect 40/40 score from respected Japanese magazine *Famitsu*.[21] According to professional reviewers in the specialist press at least, *Ocarina of Time* is the closest thing to the perfect videogame currently witnessed. The sheer number of fansites dedicated to producing art, stories and even games based on the Zelda universe stands as a testament to the game's commercial as well as critical success and the depth of feeling that players still feel for the games today.[22]

Yet herein we glimpse part of the problem. *Ocarina of Time*'s perfect score is a little misleading in that it is almost impossible to treat this as a game that sits alone in isolation. As part of an already well-loved series that,

The Legend of Zelda: Ocarina of Time: the perfect videogame?

along with *Super Mario* and *Metroid*, practically embodies Nintendo and their approach to videogames, *Ocarina of Time* has a past and at least part of the pleasure of play derives from the fact that familiar but different settings, characters and gameplay mechanics are filtered through new technologies, granted new graphics and sound, and afforded new methods of control, input and output. *Ocarina of Time* succeeds to some extent because it is old and new in perfect synthesis. It takes the best of classic game design and combines it with 3D visuals, a beautiful interactive soundtrack and a new joypad that offers unparalleled control and connection with the gameworld.

Of course, none of this should lead us to consider *Ocarina of Time* as simply a '*Legend of Zelda* Greatest Hits' or a remastered, enhanced version of the previous games. In the finest tradition of Miyamoto's other landmark titles, such as *Super Mario Bros*, *Super Mario 64* and *Nintendogs*, *Ocarina of Time* is brimming with invention and innovation and at almost every turn the player encounters an idea so novel that many other developers would base an entire game design around it. The control system with its mapping of hardware buttons to icons on screen so that the player is never confused by an opaque interface; the z-targeting that allows players to 'lock on' to enemies and strafe around them remains the most elegant solution to the problem of 3D combat; the use of masks and the titular ocarina with its array of tunes that can be acquired, learned and performed to bring about elemental changes such as turning day to night, are just some of the myriad flashes of game design genius that *Ocarina of Time* is suffused with. Perhaps more than any feature, though, it is the ability to move through time that marks out the game as a masterpiece. Time travelling is not a causal game mechanic and the consequences of actions and decisions performed in the past are significant and meaningful. Even the seemingly innocent planting of a seed is lent importance as the tree that subsequently grows from it in the future may make certain areas accessible if climbed, for example. The gameplay has a depth that few titles even approach and that is only really revealed in its full glory when consulting the walkthroughs and FAQs of master players.[23]

But *Ocarina of Time* is broad as well as deep and there is such extraordinary variety in the gameplay that it is difficult to characterise the game. This is due to the enormous number of sidequests in the game. While the primary objective of the game is dictated by the rescue plot that sees the player as a young boy named Link charged with freeing Princess Zelda from the clutches of the evil Ganondorf, much of the play time is spent engaged in activities that are perhaps only peripheral to this central narrative. This structure and its inherent non-linearity offer the player an extraordinary sense of freedom and it is rare to feel hemmed in by the game or that one is being pushed along a predefined pathway. The sense of freedom is reinforced spatially as *Ocarina of Time*'s gameworld is arranged as a coherent and contiguous environment with each differently themed dungeon, village, mountain or castle linked by the expansive overworld of Hyrule Field. Traversing this world with the trusty steed Epona, there is a palpable sense of being-in-the-world. And although it is a hostile place under the spell of evil, there is good here and allies, buoyed by the courage that you show in your quest, offer their help along the way. Above all, this is a familiar world. The world of Zelda, of Link, of Nintendo, of the golden age of videogames. Perfect.

19. <www.metacritic.com/games/platforms/n64/legendofzeldaocarina>.

20. <www.gamerankings.com/htmlpages2/197771.asp>.

21. <www.famitsu.com>.

22. See Zelda Universe's list of fansites, for example, at
    <www.zeldauniverse.net/component/option,com_weblinks/catid,2/Itemid,63/>.

23. See the many *Ocarina of Time* walkthroughs and guides available at GameFAQs.
    <www.gamefaqs.com/console/n64/game/197771.html>.

Publisher: Nintendo; **Platform**: Nintendo 64.

The Legend of Zelda: The Wind Waker
2003
Nintendo

If ever one needed evidence for the passion and feeling that players have for their favourite games, *The Legend of Zelda: The Wind Waker* would be the obvious place to start enquiries. The background to the case seems routine enough. Over the past twenty-five years, Nintendo have built up a legion of fiercely devoted fans by producing a slew of innovative game designs with endearing and enduring characters. In *The Legend of Zelda*, this already well-loved company has one of its most famous, popular and commercially successful game series. Eclipsed only by the antics of a certain moustachioed, overall-clad plumber, the *Zelda* series commands the loyalty of players the world over who dedicate enormous amounts of their time and energy exploring the worlds of the game, talking to every last character, no matter how inconsequential, undertaking every last sidequest and trading sequence, no matter how trivial and unrelated to the principal objective of the game, just to 'complete' the experience. On countless fan-produced websites littered across the web, avid players and learned elders discuss the minutiae of the individual titles that comprise the *Zelda* canon, debating the larger chronology that the playable episodes offer us in only fleetingly tantalising glimpses. The artistic followers of *Zelda*, perhaps less able, perhaps less interested in the scholarly study of the lore and histories of the *Legend*, pay homage in their own way with pictures that reimagine the characters and worlds, and stories that extend the fables into the past and future. Some even dare to create their own *Zelda*-inspired games. Why dare? Because *The Legend of Zelda* is not merely a videogame, not merely a great videogame, not even a great Nintendo videogame. *The Legend of Zelda* is a Miyamoto videogame. Shigeru Miyamoto's legend is writ even larger in the history of Nintendo than *Zelda*'s. Creator of some of the most important and influential characters and game designs, including *Super Mario* and *Metroid*, in recent years

Miyamoto has become as much a corporate mascot as his inventions. Routinely wheeled out at development conferences and trade shows to rapturous applause, the man can apparently do no wrong, even employed by Nintendo to lay his healing hands on the works in progress of other developers and set them back on the path. Every game he touches turns to gold and fans eager to devour the latest, and presumably greatest, instalment of the *Zelda* series could hardly wait for the first screenshots or movies of the game, and forums and newsgroups buzzed with anticipation. Make no mistake, this is a well-loved videogame handed down to players by the most revered of developers. With a new, super-powerful console promising an almost unimaginable graphical leap forward from the last iteration, what would Miyamoto do?

Two words. Cel shading. Two responses. Love or hate.

To say that the decision to shift from a 'realistic' graphical style to a self-consciously cartoon-like aesthetic with bright, flat-shaded surfaces in bold colours and thick black outlines as though hand drawn with a Rotring divided the *Zelda* fanbase is more than an understatement. Deliberately and even successfully artful though it may have been, for many diehards, this simply was not *Zelda*. As one clearly dismayed fan reported to the *Zelda* Guide fan website on 12 March 2002:

> I don't understand Nintendo's decision. I read an interview with Miyamotto and he said they had plenty of different ideas for the game style. I find it really hard to believe this was the best decision. I mean think about it . . . Zelda has always been a serious adventure style game. They made it look like some kids are gonna pop up and start singing Barney songs . . . Nintendo will realize this when it comes out and they see the sales results. I think this decision has turned every hardcore lover of the series away.

> (Cited in Newman, 2004)

The sense of betrayal is palpable and this is before anybody has even played the game. Screenshots in magazines and on websites and short movie clips of gameplay footage were all it took to polarise this once united community of believers. The devoted remained true to Miyamoto, placing their continued trust in Nintendo's auteur and their gaming god and treating this as a test of their faith.

In the end, for all the furore, *The Wind Waker* stayed remarkably true to the gameplay mechanics and design of the series and the game notched up reviews that, although perhaps inevitably falling some way short of the rapture that greeted *Ocarina of Time*, were respectable and would no doubt be the envy of many other developers.

Whether or not the sales charts vindicated or chastened Nintendo is, as usual, difficult to say given the videogame industry's reluctance to present straightforward sales figures, preferring to muddy the waters with details of 'shipped units' that take no account of remaindered or returned inventory, for example. The decision to return to the previous aesthetic style for the forthcoming GameCube/Wii *Zelda* title (*The Twilight Princess*) will doubtless be seen by some as an admission of guilt on Nintendo's part and of Miyamoto's fallibility, though those with keener eyes on the forthcoming release schedules will note that the upcoming DS title *The Legend of Zelda: The Phantom Hourglass* is to be presented in glorious – or is that notorious – cel shading.

Publisher: Nintendo; **Platform**: Nintendo GameCube.

Lego Star Wars: The Video Game
2005
Traveller's Tales and Giant Entertainment

Lego Star Wars is a most unexpected videogame. It is unashamedly a children's game but it is among the most rewarding experiences that any player of any age can have. There is no doubt that aesthetically this is a joyous game that revels in the opportunity that it has been afforded – to play with *Star Wars*. Whether they are a fan of the Episodes I–III prequel movies or not, surely anybody who fails to raise a smile at the sight of quite beautifully realised and animated characters from the *Star Wars* universe bounding across the screen is a heartless person indeed. But though the audiovisual spectacle is matchless, there is far more to *Lego Star Wars* than graphics and sound. This is probably the most comprehensively playful videogame. It is so full of potential to explore and not only play but play *with* the environment, characters and scenarios. All of this is handled with that rarest quality in the world of videogames, wit, and while it deals with an American intellectual property built from Danish blocks, this is a quintessentially English game. Confident and self-assured perhaps, but only because it is so certain of its quality. Subtle, reserved and refined, *Lego Star Wars* is a masterpiece of contemporary videogame design.

What is so interesting, however, is that it was designed principally for children. Yet, in their quest for a game design and mechanic that will enable children's play, Traveller's Tales and Giant seem to have discovered the secret of what makes videogame play fun for anybody. Maybe we were all just big kids all along, or maybe game design has built-in tropes and norms that we have not had the confidence or opportunity to challenge. Take the way *Lego Star Wars* deals with death. This is not a metaphysical question, but one about game design and genre conventions. Over the last few decades, videogames have been built around a mechanic that sees the player offered a finite number of 'tries' or 'lives' to complete specific sections, levels or sequences. Lose all your lives and the game ends. Indeed, such is the pervasiveness of this mechanic that it has become a prime means of managing difficulty and challenge in videogames and risk is offset against the possibility of losing a life and edging ever closer to Game Over. The solution to this problem is beautifully simple. Do away with 'lives' and make the player feel safe.

Now, safety might not seem like the kind of word normally associated with videogames, and certainly does not sound like the way to create compelling or exhilarating gameplay, yet this is precisely what *Lego Star Wars* offers. Getting blasted by an enemy does not end the game but rather sees one's character disintegrate into its constituent blocks. Elegant and witty as this is, what is most important is that instead of forcing the player to restart the level or stage from the beginning, here the player is simply pushed back a few steps down the path already travelled. So, there is a penalty but it is not severe and does not dissuade experimentation, exploration or act as discouragement. Devised as a means of encouraging younger players to keep moving forward, it transpires that this mechanic is extremely rewarding regardless and ensures that fun is maintained throughout.

So far, we have only considered the pleasures a solitary player might derive from *Lego Star Wars*. However, its coup de grâce is in its multiplayer mode. Typically, simultaneous multiplayer gaming is competitive. One player tries to beat the other, perhaps on a race track, or perhaps quite literally with fists or weapons. *Lego Star Wars*' multiplayer mode helps add the word co-operation to the gaming lexicon. Simultaneous two-player co-operative play offers more than twice the fun of the single-player game. Battling together, effortlessly fending off laser blasts with a deft twirl of the light sabre, is uplifting and any child, of any age, will want to make this the standard mode of play. Of course, this is not always possible. Parents are not always available to play when their children demand, or for as long, nor can children always be relied upon to want to play when its suits their parents . . . To counter this, *Lego Star Wars* does not build separate and discrete single-player and multiplayer modes that offer exclusive pleasures for one or two players. Rather, a second player can drop in and out of a game at any time and so, at any moment, a single-player game can become a co-operative multiplayer extravaganza.

Boasting truly innovative design features, expertly executed with an infectious enthusiasm and relish, *Lego Star Wars* is one videogame that players of every age should play yet many may overlook because of its apparently child-centred advertising and marketing campaign. The recently announced sequel that offers the altogether more tantalising possibility of playing in the universe of the original *Star Wars* Trilogy, which so many thirty-somethings grew up with and that made such an enormous impact on popular culture, will surely help ensure that *Lego Star Wars* finds the wide audience it deserves.

Publisher: Eidos Interactive; **Platform**: Sony PlayStation 2, Microsoft Xbox, GameCube, PC.

Lemmings
1991
DMA Design

It's rare that videogames are as benevolent as this. A glance through gaming history reveals thousands of titles that demand destruction or violence, yet very few which charge the player with having to care about the welfare of others. *Lemmings* offered Amiga players a wholly new paradigm of play in its core concept – *preserve* the lives of the eponymous lemmings.

As up to a hundred of the creatures relentlessly stream into the level, the player must create a safe passage for them to the exit gateway. The single-screen worlds, are, of course, full of danger; chasms, lava, water are all present in abundance, and all will instantly end the life of any lemming. Rather than control any individual lemming, the player is enabled to give certain lemmings special skills that, when invoked, play their part in building the solution. For example, a lemming might be blocker (causes all lemmings that reach it to turn around and walk back the way they came), a digger (tunnels vertically down until it reaches air) or a bomber (counts to five and explodes, killing itself but blowing a hole in the terrain it is near). These and other skills must be used together to get your lemmings out. There will, however, be sacrifices – each level demands only you save a certain percentage of the overall lemming population. Some must usually die for the greater good and the game makes great play in attempting to extract as much sympathy as possible from the player for each death. It is a cold-hearted player that can't feel some bond with them; the lemmings are amusingly cute.

As an exercise in graphical economy, *Lemmings* is outstanding. Apparently born out of a studio argument about how small an effective character animation could be, Mike Dailly argued 8x8 pixels and created a lemming animation to prove the point. The weight of characterisation that the animation achieves is remarkable and comes into its most manipulative best at the point of death, particularly by group explosion.

Should a level prove unconquerable by the current player tactics, it is for the player themselves to decide when to give up. This is not achieved by a simple 'quit' button however; rather the player must invoke the 'nuke' command, whereupon a countdown appears over their heads. Moments before their demise, they emit a weak 'Oh no!' before rapidly exploding.

The intentional modesty of the visual design and the simplicity of the core game led to *Lemmings* being ported to virtually every major gaming system released. Most recently, the game has found a new lease of life on handheld platforms such as PSP with an EyeToy version tantalisingly promised.

Publisher: Psygnosis; **Platform**: Commodore Amiga.

Little Computer People
1985
Activision Inc.

Given the extraordinary success and visibility of *The Sims*, the idea of a videogame centring on caring for and communicating with the inhabitants of a virtual world inside a PC might not seem especially novel. Observing and influencing the behaviour of relatively autonomous cyberbeings as they go about their daily business has become a routine part of the lives of millions of PC and console owners over the last few years. But, Activision's *Little Computer People* predates the new *Sim*-pretenders by decades. Twenty-one years ago, Activision encouraged a generation of Commodore 64 gamers more used to platforms games and shoot-em-ups to turn their attentions on the inner workings of the machine, where strange things lurked . . .

> As you may have read, we suspected for quite some time that there was something living inside most computers . . . We now believe that every single computer has its own Little Computer Person. And that every LCP is unique in appearance and personality. This is why we have opened up the research project to all interested computer owners.

So begins the Letter of Introduction from David Crane and Sam Nelson included in *A Computer Owner's Guide To The Care Of And Communication With LITTLE COMPUTER PEOPLE*. No instruction manual here. This is a research project, after all. The *Guide* was part of a lavish package that, importantly, included the game itself – or rather the 'House on a Disk', as it was known to members of the Activision *Little Computer People* Research Group. Upon first booting up the program, the player – or researcher – is presented with a project notebook into which they enter their name along with the date and time. The notebook automatically updates to record progress, keeping track, for example, of the number of encounters with the research subject. Although, at first, the subject is conspicuously absent and the researcher finds themselves staring at a screen displaying nothing but an empty house for a few agonising minutes, such is the reliability of Commodore 64 games, particularly those on floppy disks, that this could easily be yet another crash. However, patience is rewarded and, before long, but long before Big Brother, a Little Computer Person moves into the house. And, sure enough, just as the Activision *Little Computer People* Research Group claim, no two LCPs are the same. Names are chosen from a list of 256 (in fact, the final list is only 252 because of a transcription error[24]) and personalities and appearances are assembled from random variables that, surprisingly, occur because every C64 disk was actually unique – duplicated with a exclusive serial number embedded in the code.[25]

Once ensconced in their new home, the LCP (and the dog that always accompanies them) goes about their chores, occasionally entertaining themselves at the piano or with good book, or performing their necessary daily ablutions. Part of the pleasure for the researcher is precisely the same as the voyeuristic viewer of reality TV, yet here there is also a direct chance to interact with the action (and through this action, ultimately undermining the integrity of the research project). Deliveries of books, records, food and water (for the LCP and their dog) can be arranged through simple key presses, and a series of keyword text inputs, much like that employed in text adventures, can prompt the LCP into action: 'please dance', 'please feed the dog'.

For all its scholarly intentions, *Little Computer People* avoids didacticism, although the budding researcher will soon learn the benefit of courtesy as any request prefaced by a simple 'please' is a sure-fire way to improve the LCP's mood. They can even play games with their new-found friend – 'Card War', 'Anagrams' and '5-Card Draw Poker' – though winning is not always desirable as LCPs are rather bad losers. If the objective of *Little Computer People* is to keep the LCP happy, then this is a game that it is best, and most honourable, to lose. All in the name of research, of course.

24. See <www.the-commodore-zone.com/legends/crane/crane.htm>.

25. David Crane explains the uniqueness of each C64 disk at
    <www.softpres.org/?id=article:game:little_computer_people>.

Publisher: Activision Inc.; **Platform**: Commodore 64.

Lumines: Puzzle Fusion
2004
Q Entertainment

Superficially, *Lumines*[26] bears many similarities to *Fantavision*. Both are puzzle games, both were European launch titles for new Sony hardware, and neither seem to exploit the unique selling points of their host systems. Just as *Fantavision* offered thoughtful and understated puzzling rather than emotional intensity or an interactive movie, *Lumines* is resolutely 2D despite the PSP's 3D graphics credentials and its promise to bring, for the first time, the complexity and expansiveness of PS2 gameworlds to handheld systems. Unlike *Fantavision*, however, *Lumines* has received more critical acclaim and enjoyed considerable commercial success, shipping more than half a million copies within its first year of availability.[27]

On the face of it, *Lumines* is a falling block puzzle, in the mould of venerable handheld classics like *Tetris* or *Puyo Puyo*, and of the kind that players have become used to seeing not only on home consoles and handhelds, but also online as Flash games and even on mobile phones. Blocks comprising four squares of just two colours fall relentlessly into a play area that is rendered in widescreen taking advantage of the PSP's screen aspect ratio and, much like *Tetris*, the player is engaged in a constant battle to keep the play area clear by rotating, arranging and dropping blocks so that they form same-colour sections that magically disappear as a timeline sweeps across the screen. Essentially, the game is reducible to pattern recognition and privileges spatial awareness and cognition and, without doubt, there is much complexity and depth to the gameplay despite the apparently simple ruleset and limited range of options for the player – move, rotate and drop. Indeed, players have dedicated considerable effort in establishing principles and strategies for play including separating the play area into different sections to deal with different types of blocks or even formulating 'deterministic' methods of tackling the puzzles.[28]

However, none of this captures *Lumines'* uniqueness. While the spatial gameplay may seem fundamentally visual, it is the game's audio that is particularly notable. As with creator Tetsuya Mizuguchi's previous titles, such as *Rez* and *Space Channel 5*, music does not simply underscore the action but rather is integrated into the gameplay and, to some extent, co-created by the player, indeed in discussing the inspiration for *Lumines*, Mizuguchi has described the PSP as an 'interactive walkman'.[29] The most obvious manifestation of the sonic dimensions of the game is found in the timeline that clears blocks by rhythmically sweeping from left to right across the screen, much like an audio sequencer. This timeline renders the play area both spatially and temporally delimited – it is a grid that offers limited places to drop and stack blocks but because it is a musical bar in duration the player has to deal with the space in time with the music that beats along. As such, music not only sets the pace of the game but also defines the usefulness of the game's space – truly 4D play.

As each theme's tempo changes, it follows that so too does the pace of the game and the demands on the player. Moreover, every movement of a block is accompanied by a musical sound that complements the level's theme, so moving, dropping and rotating blocks adds to *Lumines'* sonic soundscape, while each theme is itself broken down into a series of loops that may be advanced, sustained or layered, depending on the player's overall performance. Large clearances of blocks lead to a crescendo that advances the tune, for example. Where *Electroplankton* is a musical performance environment to play with, to play *Lumines* is to remix through pattern-matching, puzzling and gaming.

Unlocking new combinations of music and visuals (known as 'skins' in the game) is one objective of the single-player mode and unusually for a puzzle game – especially for a handheld system – play sessions may last in excess of an hour. Two-player modes make use of wireless connectivity and see further comparisons with *Fantavision* in its use of a moving dividing line separating each player's available time/space within the play area.

To reflect its synthesis of music and gameplay, in Europe, *Lumines* is subtitled *Puzzle Fusion* while in Japan, it is known as *Puzzle x Music*.

26. In interviews, creator Tetsuya Mizuguchi indicates that the game's name is pronounced 'luminous' and plays on the phoenetic pronunciation of the Katakana spelling of the name in Japanese (for more, see <www.lumines.jp>).
27. <mizuguchi.biz/2005/10/post_187.php>.
28. For example, see *gmasterflash*'s guide at <www.gamefaqs.com/portable/psp/game/924594.html>.
29. See <www.gamespot.com/psp/puzzle/lumines/download_ini.html?sid= 6115035&mode=previews>.

Publisher: Ubisoft/Bandai; **Platform**: Sony PlayStation Portable.

Manhunt
2003
Rockstar North

There has been an enormous amount written about *Manhunt*. Perhaps more than any other videogame, it has filled the column inches of editorials, features and letters pages of not only specialist gaming publications but also the mainstream press so often indifferent to or even disinterested in videogames. And yet, for all the page upon page of copy, little has been written about the actual game itself and so, while many will know of the game, few will be able to describe its premise, its gameplay, or its substance and content. The reason is that *Manhunt* is discussed almost exclusively in terms of its consequences – and specifically in terms of the harmful and damaging nature of its 'effects' on the attitudes and behaviour of its players. Although it is by no means the first videogame to be vilified in this manner, just as videogames are by no means the first popular media form to be publicly criticised and blamed for social and cultural ills, it has achieved an extraordinary notoriety that belies its status as a marginal title of little interest or importance within the canon of videogames.

Upon its initial release in 2003, Rockstar North's game met with a fairly muted reception. It was received reasonably well by professional reviewers and critics but sales charts told a rather different story and the game made little significant impact. Certainly, those who had become accustomed to Rockstar's previous titles, and in particular the *Grand Theft Auto* series, were left disappointed by the promotion of style over substance and the repetitive gameplay lacking in innovation and invention. Moreover, *Manhunt* was utterly lacking in the wit and humour that had come to characterise Rockstar's published work to date. *Manhunt* centres around killing. Vicious beatings are meted out in increasingly graphic, ultraviolent ways with ever more gruesome weaponry and paraphernalia ranging from the at-hand carrier bag to the rather more premeditated chainsaw. This is not, however, unmotivated or indiscriminate killing. As a

Manhunt: Rockstar's ultraviolence courted controversy but did little to advance the debate on videogame violence

prisoner saved from Death Row, the player is ordered by the voice of the unseen character to whom they owe their liberty to commit various acts of violence. The disembodied voice is, in fact, a 'director', literally orchestrating the action and building scenes for what is assumed to be a 'snuff movie' created for their own, sometimes self-evident, pleasure and gratification. This grisly premise is reinforced in the game's aesthetic, which is all dim, shadowy lighting, urban decay and is replete with the scarring of gangland territory wars. There can be no doubt whatsoever that *Manhunt* is a thoroughly unpleasant videogame though, despite its concentrated and unflinching representations of aggression and brutality, its content is not out of step with the stuff of many mainstream movies on general release and it was duly awarded its 18 certification by the BBFC.

What propelled the game into the public consciousness was the accusation that it was indirectly responsible for the murder of a fourteen-year-old boy, Stefan Pakeerah, in Leicester in 2004. In fact, it was the murdered boy's mother, Giselle, who made the claim, asserting that her son's killer had been inspired by the game. It would not take long before regional and national newspapers ran stories that detailed the 'copycat' behaviour and led with headlines such as 'Murder by PlayStation' (*Daily Mail*, 29 July 2004). In response, some UK high-street retailers withdrew the game from their shelves, leading to accusations of censorship from some quarters. The net result of the effective 'ban' was to drive sales of the game higher as players sought out the title from those retailers still stocking it in order to find out what the fuss was about. As such, the enormous publicity generated by the media coverage served only to heighten interest in and the visibility of the product itself.

As the story developed, it transpired that Leicestershire Police had discounted the possibility of a link to the game at the very outset of their investigation and discussion turned away from the specifics of *Manhunt* and to the media effects claim, with journalists, academics and players adding their voices. There remains no definitive or simple answer to the question of media effects or influence with scholars and critics from different disciplines vehemently arguing at each extreme of the debate (see Cumberbatch, 1998; 2004; Newman and Oram, 2006). What is particularly lamentable is the videogames industry's reluctance, or perhaps even inability, to take part in this debate. Instead, the industry fell back on trade bodies such as ELSPA (European Leisure Software Producers Association) and the frankly rather tired position on certification and age-ratings that suggested that these children should, simply, not have been allowed to access or play this game. Had there been an informed, open debate on media violence, effects and influences, then at least there might have been some silver lining to the tragic events surrounding Stefan Pakeerah's death. Instead, the popular and specialist press retreated all too easily into their polarised stances of blame and defence and the ensuing furore served only to confuse players further and disallow the possibility of discussion and analysis. It would not be fair to suggest that *Manhunt* itself has held back the debates about games and their role in contemporary society and popular culture, but the manner in which the public discussion panned out exposes the ignorance about gaming as a medium and as a media form and exposes the poverty of the critical language available to describe and codify this most pervasive of entertainment media.

Publisher: Rockstar Games; **Platform**: Sony PlayStation 2, Microsoft Xbox, PC.

Mercenary (Escape from Targ)
1985
Paul Woakes

One of the most overlooked gems of the 1980s, *Mercenary* and its two sequels have become the object of great and sustained affection among those who discovered them. Perhaps the greatest hindrance to the game achieving the commercial success it deserved was simply that it followed *Elite*. Taking place within a vector-drawn world and having a similar open-ended structure, *Mercenary* could perhaps have been read as something of a lesser, me-too title. In reality, the game is at least as rewarding as its more famous vector sci-fi predecessor, in many cases it delivers and sustains its environment more effectively. *Mercenary* was a huge critical success, with one reviewer commenting, 'I have absolutely no criticism to make of it.'[30]

The game's principal achievement was in creating a plausible sense of scale, with very little visual detail. Taking place entirely within a city on the planet Targ, the play begins with one of the first examples of an in-engine cut scene, where your ship crash lands. The exposition (and subsequent advice through the game) is provided by a scrolling text message across the bottom of the screen, otherwise known as Benson – your ninth-generation PC. Benson is revealed to be a sarcastic commentator as the game progresses.

The city within which the game takes place is incredibly sparse, and rendered entirely by wireframe vectors. To keep the speed of the game high, 'hidden' faces of buildings are not removed. The landscape has much to yield, however, in terms of architectural wit. The designer, Paul Woakes, has embedded a sense of playfulness in the very design of the city that rewards players who discover certain features. For example, an Atari logo can be discovered and destroyed – however, this creates very different consequences depending on if you're playing the game on a Commodore or Atari machine. The level of sheer graft and care evident in the game is hugely comforting to the player.

In a sadly missed convention, the game's release was followed by a separate product, the 'Targ Survival Kit'. This gifted the player with a hints guide, a fold-out map and a novella. While the current crop of hint-books serve much the same purpose, the charm and creativity often present in the format of these additional box items is sorely missed from the gaming world.

Finally, it would be doing *Mercenary* a disservice not to note its influence. While obviously following the lead established by *Elite* for open moral choices and multiple pathways towards the same goal, *Mercenary* offered players a mission-based structure by which they could earn credits for progressing throughout the game. As *EDGE* magazine noted, 'Explore a city, steal vehicles and make money from rival factions, all with a dose of humour and plenty of secrets. Sound familiar?'[31] 'GTA: Targ', indeed.

30. <www.zzap64.co.uk/zzap11/mercenary.html>.
31. *EDGE* magazine 153, September 2005.

Publisher: Novagen; **Platform**: Atari 800 XL/XE.

Metal Gear Solid
1998
Konami Computer Entertainment Japan

Metal Gear Solid is a product of the PlayStation. It was by no means the first game for Sony's console, nor was it the PlayStation per se that brought the game into existence. Unlike *WipEout*, *Metal Gear Solid*'s existence owes little to the exceptional marketing campaigns that earned the PlayStation its cachet and allowed it to ride the zeitgeist of club, drug and dance culture. Rather, this is a game that relies on the underlying technology of the console. *Metal Gear Solid* is a product of the CD-ROM. The comparatively cavernous storage that CD-ROM afforded allowed developers possibilities unimagined in previous eras where tapes, disks and cartridges were the norm. With the game program itself occupying only a small part of the available capacity, there was space aplenty for full-motion video. FMV sequences are 'pre-rendered', that is they are not drawn in real-time like the majority of game graphics but played from disk in much the same manner as video on a DVD. Because FMV can be designed and drawn on powerful computers, it is often of a subjectively higher quality than in-game graphics, and may take advantage of higher-resolution character models, richer textures and more complex lighting. In short, they more closely resemble computer-generated imagery in movies and are often directed and produced by different teams to those creating the remainder of the game. The trade-off is that FMV sequences are not 'interactive' and the player cannot influence the action they see on screen. Characters perform their actions as the director intended and the player cannot intervene or modify the course of the narrative. Games such as *Final Fantasy VII* had already made extensive use of FMV in the form of introductory movies and expositional 'cut scenes' that developed and progressed the narrative arc before placing the player back into the interactive action to perform their battle sequences. Where *Final Fantasy VII* utilised FMV to enrich the videogame, refining and advancing its aesthetic, *Metal Gear Solid*'s chief designer, Hideo Kojima, took a different approach and opted to fundamentally alter the aesthetic of the videogame. *Metal Gear Solid* is suffused with the imagery and modalities of film. Its use and mastery of dialogue, plot, camera, *mise en scène*, cinematography and characterisation are not only mature in a way that videogame players are quite unused to, but also they spill over from the FMV sequences into the interactive sections of play. In-game camera angles add to the sense of dynamism, movement and emotion, while the use of the standard game engine to render scenery and characters avoided the usual jarring shift in image quality that accompanies the move from real-time to pre-rendered graphics. By using the same quality of graphics, *Metal Gear Solid* synthesised its cut scenes and interactive gameplay, making them gel in a way unseen by players or critics. *Metal Gear Solid* was not the first videogame to attempt to push at the boundary between film and games and there is a raft of 'interactive movies' that precede it. However, if Kojima's vision is not original in its intention, it is supreme in its execution.

What is most interesting about *Metal Gear Solid*, however, is that for all its filmic intentions, it is a game that is supremely confident with its game-ness. At various points, characters draw attention to their presence in a videogame, or even to the paraphernalia of videogames hardware and interface. Where intuition might tell us that rendering the interface transparent or even invisible might be the most effective means of creating immersion or presence in the narrative and world of the game, Kojima and his team brazenly remind the player of the constructedness of this experience. This is postmodern media in playable form. Of particular note are the episodes in which enemies 'mind read' by scanning the player's memory card, or seem to display an almost machine-like ability to predict the player's every move necessitating the changing of the joypad from port one to two to thwart their efforts. This is a game full of inventive moments that play with the very idea of the videogame as a structure, as an activity and as a form. From vibrating joypads that in-game enemies control with their telekinesis to assailants who can interfere with the link between PlayStation and TV screen and turn the screen black making the player fear that the game has crashed, this is a team of developers clearly enjoying the process of making videogames (see Newman, 2002).

Metal Gear Solid has become a key franchise for Konami and, while sequels and prequels have been converted to Nintendo and Microsoft consoles, it remains a key title in Sony's line-up with *Metal Gear Solid 4: Sons of Liberty* forming a key component of the PlayStation 3 pre-launch marketing bonanza.

Publisher: Konami; **Platform**: Sony PlayStation.

Meteos
2005
Q Entertainment

Released in 2005 for Nintendo DS, *Meteos* is a puzzle game that combines elements of *Tetris*, *Columns* and *Zoo Keeper*. While it can be played with the standard D-pad and buttons, *Meteos* makes excellent use of the touch screen and, like *Yoshi Touch & Go* and *WarioWare Touched!*, can be played solely with the stylus, adding greatly to the sense of physical connection with the game. Though both of the DS's dual screens are used, the game essentially takes place on the lower display with the upper being reserved for animations and score information that come into play mostly in the breaks between levels.

In reviews, *Meteos* is invariably discussed alongside *Lumines*, largely because both titles are abstract puzzlers and were developed by Q Entertainment studios (though *Lumines*' chief developer Tetsuya Mizuguchi acted as producer on *Meteos* with lead developer duties falling to Masahiro Sakurai, whose previous credits include the Nintendo beat-em-up *Super Smash Bros*). However, these similarities notwithstanding, the two games are really quite unalike and do not stand sustained comparison. *Lumines* is a thoughtful, almost relaxingly trance-like experience that demands sensitivity to the changing rhythms of the game and implicates the player as remixer in its audiovisual world. In seeking to create an 'interactive Walkman' of the PSP, *Lumines* clearly has intentions to be 'more than just a game'. *Meteos*, on the other hand, is nothing more or less than a celebration of gaming. No media arts pretensions here, just pure, intense, twitch gaming that privileges reflexes and reactions, and that bombards the senses in the most unforgiving and unsubtle fashion.

Enjoying a preposterous backstory involving the evil planet *Meteos* destroying civilisations by sending barrages of energy, the player is charged with the task of travelling to each of the planets under attack, repelling the strike, and thereby saving the universe. Conveniently for

Sakurai and the player, planet Meteos's interplanetary assault takes the form of a series of descending coloured squares that drop into a play area. When the blocks reach the top of the screen, the planet is lost. Foiling the onslaught is as simple as lining up three or more blocks of the same colour – sure enough, this is *another* falling block puzzle game. But what sets this apart from the myriad games in this genre is the sheer speed at which the game is played. From the very outset, blocks rain down from space at an alarming rate – only after completing over a hundred lines do *Tetris*'s tetraminoes fall anywhere near this rapidly. The effect is much like a garish, multicoloured version of the *Matrix*'s opening credits where text slips down the screen in the style of a computer virus – only here, we are watching on fast-forward.

As blocks fall into parallel stacks, the player has to use the stylus to grab and drag them up and down to make horizontal or vertical lines of the same colour. Where cleared blocks in *Tetris* or *Lumines* simply disappear, *Meteos* again eschews understatement by having colour-matched lines sprout rockets and noisily blast up the screen. The variable effects of gravity on each planet mean that the jet-propelled blocks may not fire fully off screen but the player can continue to rearrange blocks even as they ascend skyward to commence 'secondary ignitions' that jettison them yet faster and further.

While *Meteos* has received considerable critical acclaim, concern has been voiced over a potential flaw in the game design that makes it possible to succeed by blindly scrubbing the touch screen.

Publisher: Ubisoft; **Platform**: Nintendo DS.

Metroid
1986
Nintendo

Along with *The Legend of Zelda* and *Super Mario*, *Metroid* is one of
Nintendo's most valuable and enduring franchises. All three series were
first introduced in the mid-1980s in Nintendo's earliest days of home
videogame console development, yet they continue to spawn new titles
and have witnessed changes in fashions and technologies as they each
made the shift from 2D to 3D, for example. More often than not,
however, they have been responsible for instigating change in game
design and have been followed by a legion of imitators. All of which is
perhaps a little curious as, in its original incarnation, *Metroid* may not
have looked immediately remarkable from a game design perspective and
seems superficially similar to the myriad platform games that emerged in
the wake of *Super Mario Bros.* Despite its sci-fi aesthetic and complicated
backstory that sees the player attempting to deal with a newly discovered

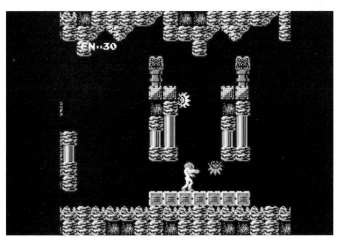

Metroid: 'He is the greatest of all the space hunters,' reads the manual. Only he was a she

and deadly lifeform assumed to have been responsible for wiping out an entire civilisation and that has been stolen by space pirates,[32] the game is apparently a 2D platform game where the objective is to traverse and conquer the complex and often hostile environment. However, there are some important differences. Where *Super Mario Bros.* presents its obstacle course as series of thematically related but spatially unconnected levels, *Metroid*'s world is contiguous and whole with missions taking place in a vast, coherent world rather than each subsequent challenge being set in a discrete level or stage. Moreover, where *Super Mario Bros.* is a one-way trip that offers the player no possibility of doubling back to re-explore the spaces already travelled, *Metroid*'s world is a maze of interconnecting passages, corridors and rooms and it is absolutely essential that players retread their steps and revisit areas. This is because regions and rooms change throughout the game, or because as enemies move through the world, for example, and because the consequences of the player's actions are sometimes to make passable what were previously dead ends, thereby opening up new areas for exploration. What we find in *Metroid* then is a game that has less in common with *Super Mario Bros.* and that bears more similarity to the gameplay and design of the *Legend of Zelda* series, with its spatially consistent world within which the player adventures and explores, and in the non-linearity of its circuitous routes through labyrinthine structures. *Metroid* has become a particular favourite of super-players who seek to play through the game in as speedy a time as possible and has spawned a community of 'speedrunners' and 'sequence breakers' who play with the game's structure, finding exploits that allow them to shave seconds off their completion times.[33]

Metroid has one more surprise up its sleeve. Cast in the role of Samus Aran, a space hunter sent by the Federation Police to destroy the Mother Brain, the storyline is by no means the game's revelation and what you do is less important that who you are. In *Metroid*'s instruction manual, Samus is described in some detail:

He is the greatest of all the space hunters and has successfully completed numerous missions that everybody thought were absolutely impossible. He is a cyborg: his entire body has been surgically strengthened with robotics, giving him superpowers. Even the space pirates fear his space suit, which can absorb any enemy's power. But his true form is shrouded in mystery.

Mystery indeed, and on completing the game, the player learns that Samus is, in fact, a woman. Coming seven years after Ridley Scott's *Alien*, this might not seem especially novel, but if we consider the representation of women in videogames at that point, we find that any deviation from the damsel in distress/princess in need of rescue is noteworthy. Coming a decade before Lara Croft, much has been made of *Metroid*'s enlightened approach yet it is worth remembering that the player's 'reward' for completing the game quickly is a final screen showing Samus in a pink bikini. Unfortunately, in space no one can hear you scream 'girl power'.

32. See the full text from the original *Metroid* instruction manual at the 'Metroid Database', <mdb.classicgaming.gamespy.com/m1/m1manual.txt>.
33. For more on speedrunning and sequence breaking, see Newman (2005) and also 'Speed Demos Archive' at <speeddemosarchive.com/Metroid.html> and 'Metroid 2002' at <www.metroid2002.com>.

Publisher: Nintendo; **Platform**: Nintendo Entertainment System.

Microsoft Flight Simulator
1982
Microsoft Game Studios

Few genres of interactive entertainment expose the tension between simulation and game as much as flight simulators. Whereas mass-market *Sim* titles could offer us a model of urban planning that few could call into question, the flight-sim had to face the high demands for precision and accuracy from a community of pilots from inception. *MFS* was conceived and developed with this authenticity in mind.

Originally suggested by a masters thesis being completed by Bruce Chatwick in 1975, 'A Versatile Computer-Generated Dynamic Flight Display' – which demonstrated that popular computers of the day were equipped to simulate the physics of flight and provide graphical representation of it – the original became one of the best-selling titles for the Apple II machine. Microsoft moved in to exclusively license the game for the then forthcoming IBM-PC in 1981, and the franchise was born. It quickly became one of the defining titles of Windows gaming.

As the core simulation mechanic has been improved over the years, the game has presented an ever more realistic experience – one that has often been mirrored in elaborate set-ups in people's home gaming rooms. Many of the more extreme examples of this practice, with their multi-monitor displays and bespoke controller systems, come frighteningly close to creating an accurate physical cockpit itself. The visual quality of the simulation is predictably easy to track, as the fidelity of both the landscapes and the planes improves exponentially with the technology.

Perhaps most importantly, however, *MFS* can be traced as one of the pioneering sites of modding culture, which we might more usually associate with FPS titles such as *DOOM*. Constructed around an open structure, which allowed third parties to create their own models for almost any element of the game, a prolific community of modders emerged, both hobbyist and commercial. Pilots found themselves able to not just upgrade their planes, but perhaps even download and expand their simulation to include their own locale to fly through.

The draw towards game has been ever present, however, and in subsequent releases the structured mission has become more and more visible. In particular the recent E3 trailers for the forthcoming new version, *Microsoft Flight Simulator X*, focused heavily on the excitement of the air rescue. *MFS* can be a game when it wants to be, but at its heart will always be the complex rules of flight – keeping it marginalised to the (albeit very large) personal computer audience. Microsoft went on to release *Microsoft Train Simulator* and *Microsoft Space Simulator* to lesser commercial effect.

Publisher: Microsoft; **Platform**: PC.

MineSweeper
1991 (Windows 3.x)
Robert Donner

With the exception perhaps of the Nokia mobile phone version of *Snake*, few games can boast to have achieved the level of ubiquity of *MineSweeper*. Dominating the casual games market before marketeers had even recognised such a thing existed, the game has passed into the small and elite class of videogames played regularly by people who 'don't play videogames'. Indeed, in its very embeddedness in the Windows operating system environment (alongside 'FreeCell') it is often not viewed as a videogame at all, but merely a welcome and entertaining diversion built into the desktop world in which so many people spend their working lives. While the precise moment of creation is shrouded in time, with versions being traced back at least as far as 1981, it is widely accepted as truly reaching the mainstream with Donner's version of 1989.

The game itself is built around a deceptively simple premise, which, while leaning heavily on the player's ability to deduce probabilities, is occasionally unable to be played without resorting to some element of total chance. There is, thus, some discussion as to the existence of the possibility of a 'perfect game' of *MineSweeper*. The limits of this author's understanding of statistical analysis prevents credible discussion of the detail of the game's nuances, but a brief trawl of the Internet will yield an extraordinary community of *MineSweeper* enthusiasts and commentators.

With its basic mechanic so transferable and suggestive to subtle (and not so subtle) tweaking, the game has spawned a long line of similar entrants in its family. As well as versions for most operating systems, further skews have included against-the-clock trials, competitive network *MineSweeper* and the particularly challenging 3D version.

Publisher: Microsoft Game Studios (a version of MineSweeper is included with Windows versions 3.x–XP); **Platform**: PC.

Mr Do!
1982
Taito

You are a clown. Dressed from head to toe in full Motley, you have an insatiable craving for the cherries that grow, inexplicably, underground in small groves. Scrabbling through the soil in search of the succulent, fruity booty, clearing the dirt with your bare hands such are the depths of your desire, your journey to Pick-Your-Own heaven is hindered only by the army of ill-tempered monsters that patrol this underground realm. They guard the cherries – for whom we never find out – and, while they are seemingly able to resist the juicy temptation themselves, they are inevitably hungry for clown flesh and will cheerfully gobble any Fool foolish enough to cross their path. Fortunately, in addition to a suit bedecked with pom-poms, you are equipped with a bouncing ball – a bouncing ball that destroys clown-eating monsters on contact, mercifully. Of course, it would be ridiculous to think that a magical bouncing ball would be the only tool at your disposal. You could always drop a giant apple on the heads of the monsters to squish them flat. The apples grow underground too but it goes without saying that they hold no culinary or nutritional interest for a cherry-obsessed clown. Apples are weapons. Just hope that one of the five Alphamonsters, whose bellies are each embellished with one letter of the word EXTRA and who once dispatched in toto extend your life, don't descend into the cherry grove. They and their small entourage of munching meanies love apples and will chomp them down whole, putting your weaponry well and truly out of reach.

All of this could easily be the product of a kind of hallucinogenic experiment that would likely have seen Timothy Leary checking into The Priory. However, this is no 1960s loved-up trip. This is the world of *Mr Do!*. While the preposterous surrealism of the scenario, the eyewateringly vivid visuals and unapologetic jollity of the sound effects and music are the most immediately striking elements of the game, delving a little deeper, *Mr Do!* reveals some interesting and innovative design. At first glance, Taito's game might appear to be little more than a *Pac-Man*

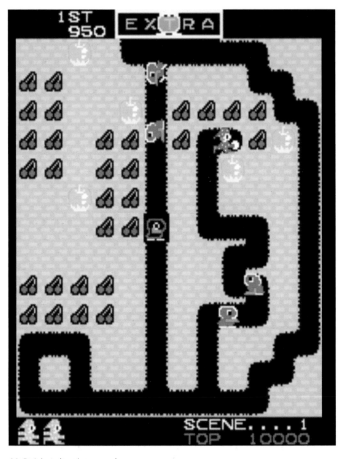

Mr Do!: just clowning around

clone – an attempt by the *Space Invaders* creator to cash in on the extraordinary popularity of the pill-popping yellow eating machine and regain its place at the top of the development heap. Power pills become cherries, ghosts become monsters, and the clown throws a ball that looks worryingly like Pac-Man himself. But it is in the maze that *Mr Do!*'s innovation is to be found. Where *Pac-Man*'s labyrinth is fixed, *Mr Do!*'s is created during play, by the player. Even this tells only part of the story. It is the monsters' differing abilities to traverse or add to the pathways that lend the game its complexity. Mr Do! can dig but, in the main, the monsters that chase him cannot. Instead, they roam the routes created by the player's every movement as Mr Do!. And so, the very act of moving and chasing cherries creates a path that inevitably leads the monsters to . . . the player. To compound matters, as the game progresses some monsters develop the ability to shift earth themselves. Suddenly, the safety of the circuitous pathway is shattered and the monsters are digging their way straight to the player, sometimes even teaming up and cutting off exit routes. Learning that their strength is in numbers, the monsters team up to push out of their collective way apples that may have blocked their individual paths in earlier stages.

A deceptively simple game, *Mr Do!* was widely ported to consoles and home computers and while the franchise enjoyed a number of sequels and spin-offs throughout the 1980s, including *Mr Do's Castle*, which saw the clown taking on a horde of troublesome and cantankerous unicorns, and the rollercoaster-based cherry collecting fun of *Mr Do's Wild Ride*, it has not been developed in latter years. As is so often the case, the purity of the original means that it remains the best expression of the *Do!* ethos of untrammelled fun and silliness, and for those willing to look behind imagery more often associated with substance abuse there is . . . well, substance.

Publisher: Universal; **Platform**: Coin-Op.

Myst
1993
Cyan

In a world dominated by speed, exhilaration and rapid cycles of stimulus to the player, it is difficult to imagine that for many years the best-selling PC game of all time was a title that was the antithesis of these usual videogame tropes. In comparison to other games, in comparison to television – even in comparison to most screensavers (a form to which it is often compared) – *Myst* is slowness made interactive.

Its heritage is clear, emerging as it did at a time when hypertext fiction was becoming the favoured experimental platform of the academic literati, *Myst* nestled into a comfortable middle-class position. It wasn't violent, it wasn't populated by aliens – it even launched on the Apple Macintosh. If you were clever and concerned about appearing trivial, *Myst* was the game it was okay to like.

Set in a beautifully 3D rendered world, with a core narrative embedded in the kinds of imagery of books and literacy that would make Eco proud, *Myst* is conspicuous in its aspiration to be a literate, if not poetic, videogame. The idyllic paradise in which the 'action' takes place is presented in loving detail, although in many respects it was perhaps as much the content as the quality of this design that differentiated *Myst*. Players hadn't been presented with landscapes of such rich ecology in a videogame before. *Myst* was about water, foliage, sand, wood – it was at pains to create a convincing organic universe, albeit a wholly static one.

Originally constructed using Apple's Hypercard software, the game wore the tool of its authoring on its sleeve. In playing the game the sensation is that of flicking through a very beautiful collection of photographs. The game made innovative use of CD-ROM technology of the time, also embedding Quicktime movie footage into the game for exposition and action sequences. Leaning heavily on an elaborate narrative backstory and the manufacturing of its unique atmosphere, the ludic challenges involved all revolved around the solving of (occasionally incredibly complex) puzzles found within the world. It's tempting to imagine what *Myst* might be if remade now, its puzzles often reaching towards physics-based problems; it might make an interesting companion piece to work such as *Half-Life 2*.

While its pretensions have been widely ridiculed by the more traditional videogame cognoscenti, it surely deserves attention and respect for committing to its premise so completely. Few titles have proved as divisive. Never once deviating from the rhythm it establishes at its outset, its gameplay is either beguiling and hypnotic, or intolerable and dull – depending on your tastes. The index of its importance is best demonstrated by the amount of parodies constructed of it, among them *Missed*, *Pyst* and *Mylk* (which was based in the world of dairy products). It also went on to spawn a number of sequels and novels based on its world and characters.

Perhaps the greatest triumph of *Myst* is to grow the audience for videogames by extraordinary sleight of hand. Rather than deliver videogame literacy, it delivers verbiage in a videogame – it makes its players *feel* literate. For parents of gamers keen to avoid the trivialities of most mass-market titles, it presented a very attractive alternative. A safe, cosy world into which both their minds (and the minds of their gamer children) would be unchallenged by the extremities of more typical videogame fare, it flew from store shelves and into family PCs. It was a title with which the minds of our young could be trusted; indeed, it has been adopted by a number of teachers as a stimulus for discussion around its visual and narrative themes.

Publisher: Brøderbund; **Platform**: Macintosh.

N
2005
Metanet Software

The Internet is brilliant. As well as enabling the low-cost distribution of existing digital products, the technologies that have been developed specifically for it proved to be rich platforms for the creation of new work by independent game-makers. Few have been more successful than Macromedia Flash, a vector-based technology that has evolved over the years to be a powerful and open platform for game design. Relatively easy to learn the basics of, but with a powerful scripting language at your call should you require it, it has encouraged a whole new wave of 'casual' game designers to try their hand.

Metanet Software, which is comprised of Raigan Burns and Mare Sheppard, are developers with a manifesto. Fiercely independent and committed to innovation, they produce the kinds of statements (and software) that only small independent developers can afford to make. 'We believe that the relationship between marketing and game design should be either non-existent, or read-only. The purpose of marketing is to sell a product, not to design a product.'[34] This manifesto has so far produced but one game for Metanet, and it's very good.

N, their debut title, has a pure concept. 'You are a ninja. Your god-like speed, dexterity, jumping power, and reflexes are all a result of an amazingly fast metabolism; sadly, so is your natural lifetime of 1.5 minutes.' In the ninety seconds of life your character is granted, your challenge is to traverse the platforms of the level and collect all the gold you can find. When it is all found, the exit portal will open and you can make your escape. Essentially, *N* is *Manic Miner* with a sophisticated physics engine.

N takes the platform games of the early 8-bit days, with their demanding pixel-perfect jumps, and reinvents them as a fluid, flowing dance (the one exception to this is of course the sublime *Cauldron 2*, with its gently bouncing pumpkin). Your 'ninja' is but a stick figure, but flies around the screen with the grace of Nureyev. Physics have been playing an increasingly important role in recent videogames. Titles as diverse as *Half-Life 2* to *Gish* have all used gravity, buoyancy and transferred energy of various entertaining types to create new experiences of play. *N* is a polished example of a spare, focused aesthetic – its minimal visual styling drawing attention wholly to the action.

N, and its open level format, has also inspired a loyal and large collection of level-makers. The kinds of work they are creating extend far beyond simply making further levels for people to play. Most interesting are the DDA (don't do anything!) levels, in which the ninja is propelled around the level by wholly natural forces, performing an often extraordinary series of tightly choreographed stunts for the viewer. In addition to its achievements as a game in its own right, *N* is an inspirational platform for the creativity of others. Ninjas are brilliant.

34. <www.harveycartel.org/metanet/corporate/philosophy.html>.

Publisher: Metanet Software; **Platform**: Macromedia Flash.

Nintendogs
2005
Nintendo

Nintendogs is hard. Really hard. Not in the way that *Ikaruga* or *Radiant Silvergun* are hard. There are no bullets or lasers here. *Nintendogs* is hard *work*. It is time consuming, demanding and even repetitive. You might have thought that a Tamagotchi was hard work as it bleeped for food or a hosing down, but those critters were positively independent, standoffish misanthropes compared with the insistent and needy temperament of a Nintendog. Tamagotchi was highly effective in its simulation of a life dependent on you for its every need. Most amazingly, despite the crude representation of the creature in just a few monochrome pixels and all but the barest animation, it also managed to communicate character. *Nintendogs* bears some similarities to this but it is not simply an extension of the virtual pet design. This is no Tamagotchi with enhanced graphics. It is not even a dog-owning simulation. In fact, it does not feel like a simulation at all, let alone a game. This is a real dog living in your DS. A living, breathing dog. And just as it loves you, it needs you. Yes, it is extraordinarily hard work but it is also the most rewarding experience.

What moves this beyond *SimDog* is the quite extraordinary depth of character and personality of the Nintendogs. It is difficult to pinpoint exactly what it is that makes them so charming and real. Certainly, they are graphically beautiful and each breed of hound is modelled in exquisite detail, to say nothing of the animation that really is a joy to behold. Anybody whose heart does not immediately melt at the sight of three pups standing on their hind legs, jostling for position as they reach up to peer out of the screen at their new owner is a cold individual, indeed. Playtime, too, is joyous and there is an infectious look of wonder and excitement on the puppies' faces as they stride purposefully off on walkies, leap to catch the tennis ball you have thrown for them, or curiously, if a little nervously, investigate the soap bubbles you have blown. But there is much more to *Nintendogs* than admittedly exquisite graphics, fluid animation and witty gameplay vignettes. There is a magical ingredient in the mix that renders any such thoughts of 3D models completely irrelevant.

The Nintendo DS's hardware interface is at least partly responsible for the success of the game and offers the most perfect ways to not only see, but touch and even talk to your new canine chums. Rub him under his chin with the touch-sensitive screen, teach him tricks and obedience skills with your voice. No icons to click to issue instructions or long menus to select commands from – voice recognition is the key to the game. Being able to talk directly to your Nintendog creates the most visceral and seamless connection between man and beast. Such is the success of the system that it works even when it isn't working. As case in point; Nintendo demonstrated the game at a number of big screen events during 2005. In one demo, in front of a huge crowd that comprised eager teenagers and jaded games journalists, the Nintendo exec fired up the DS and in came Jimmy, a Labrador puppy. Jimmy sniffed the air, explored his surroundings and eventually walked up to the display and stared out of the screen to see what was what, clearly relishing the 'oohs' and 'aahs' that everybody initially tried to stifle but soon gave into. 'I've been training him for a while, so he knows quite a few tricks,' the demonstrator reassured the cooing masses, who would probably have been quite happy to have watched little Jimmy padding up and down minding his own business for half an hour. 'Jimmy, sit.' Nothing. 'Sit, Jimmy. Sit.' Still nothing. 'He's a little shy. Let's try again. Jimmy. S-I-T.' Jimmy wandered off, wagging his tail behind him, evidently very pleased with himself. 'Oh, Jimmy, you're so naughty.' And there was not a person in that room who didn't think, 'What a little scamp that Jimmy is. Playing up for the big crowd like that. He's always the same, you know.' Now, of course, what was really happening was the voice recognition system was not working. Jimmy is, after all, a mathematical model that triggers certain animation cycles and program routines when the console's microphone registers a waveform that near-matches a sample held in memory. The ambient noise in the auditorium (mostly wizened game hacks trying to hold back tears) meant that the game was not picking up a clear enough audio signal from Jimmy's owner/demonstrator. And so, in essence, but only because of circumstance, the game was not working. Not a great demonstration one might think but this malfunction was not merely written off because of Jimmy's cheeky, winning grin. Rather, the malfunction was not even noticed. Jimmy's charm, in part at least, came from his disobedience, his unwillingness to behave like a model, SimDog. That he did it all with a cheeky, winning grin just made you love him all the more for it. Make no mistake, Nintendogs are not well designed and animated dog models. They are dogs.

Owning and caring for a Nintendog is a rightly onerous task full of responsibility and reward. And as a piece of branding, it is exceptional. You can't say *Nintendogs* without saying Nintendo.

'Jimmy, don't do that.'

Publisher: Nintendo; **Platform**: Nintendo DS.

Osu! Tatakae! Ouendan!
2005
iNiS

The Nintendo DS is an obvious home to the rhythm game. Aside from the obvious accessibility associated with such titles (which Nintendo have been keen to promote in the past on other platforms with titles such as *Donkey Konga*) the platform itself with its touch-sensitive lower screen makes a fine percussive platform. *Osu! Tatakae! Ouendan!* is a fantastically entertaining entry into the DS rhythm-game genre, pretty much inventing the form with its release. Developers iNis, best known for the cult PS2 title *Gitaroo Man*, have delivered an extraordinarily accessible title, even in the absence of a localised English-language version. *Ouendan* (as it has become known) has found itself a strong following in import, and deservedly so.

The premise behind the game is emotively simple. The player is in control of a group of motivational cheerleaders who are called upon by characters in various forms of distress to dance them better – helping them reach their full potential. The gameplay follows the systems already established by the rhythm genre, with the player required to touch points on the screen in time to the music in moves of ever increasing complexity. Embracing the touch screen control mechanism further, as well as individual 'beats' the game also requires the player to stroke the stylus along tracks in time to the song. The skill with which these are choreographed rapidly instils in the player a feeling of musical sensitivity, an impression that they are making the music as distinct from responding to it.

The game is a triumph of visual storytelling, with each chapter opening with a synopsis of the characters' predicament underscored with a tattoo snare-drum beat (for many western audiences this cannot fail to evoke memories of the *A-Team*). Told in the fixed panels of manga (much in the style of *Trauma Center*), these feature only the most basic animation in telling their narrative. When the characters reach their point of crisis, when they can take no more they cry 'Ouendan!' and the player's role begins. The language barrier evaporates in these sequences (indeed, the only real stumbling block for a non-Japanese-reading audience is in making their initial way through the menu system) and the efficient storytelling style draws the player into the emotional world of the character.

Ouendan understands the power of popular music incredibly well, and it leverages the emotive J-pop soundtrack it employs for each character to tremendous effect. The fifteen levels of the game are fifteen songs that easily disarm the player to become an unexpectedly moving experience. Many players have reported being moved to tears at the game – it's an unusual title indeed that can so quickly and efficiently provoke such responses. Western audiences need not feel cheated for too long, however, as an English-language version of the game has been announced that uses the same mechanic but apparently different songs and narratives. We can only hope that the esoteric scenarios of the original are not dispensed with in the game's journey to a western mass market.

Publisher: Nintendo; **Platform**: Nintendo DS.

Pac-Man
1980
Namco

Even if they have not played that game itself, there can be few people with even a passing interest in popular culture who will not know the name of *Pac-Man*. Namco's ravenous yellow character became a global icon upon release in the 1980s and made the leap beyond the world of videogames to become a highly marketable, cross-media property giving rise to no end of merchandising including '*Pac-Man* Fever', a pop record penned by Buckner and Garcia.[35] At least part of the reason for the success and penetration of *Pac-Man* into wider culture circles comes not so much from the game itself or any of its structural or design qualities. Rather, in a world awash with shooting games like *Space Invaders* that placed the player at the controls of impressively armoured, but ultimately anonymous spaceships, here was an anthropomorphic character and, while he possessed only the barest of facial features, he was alive and ripe with marketing potential. The diminutive eating machine was the videogames industry's first 'cultural icon' (Bennett and Woollacott, 1987) and though he had none of these qualities in the game, he could walk and talk his way onto the side of a lunchbox, T-shirt or bedspread in a way that a mobile laser-canon simply could not. It is probably overstating matters to suggest that without *Pac-Man* there would be no *Super Mario* or any of the other raft of central humanoid videogame characters, but the dot-munching critter certainly cleared a path and did much to break the comparative stranglehold that space shooting had exerted on game design.

However, this was far from a strategic master plan executed by Namco and inspiration came in a curious manner. If *Pac-Man* seems to resemble a pizza with a slice missing, then this is because a half-eaten snack was indeed the foundation of one of the games industry's greatest creations. And so, *Pac-Man* and consumption are indissolubly linked. Not only is he one of the most voraciously consumed products of gaming

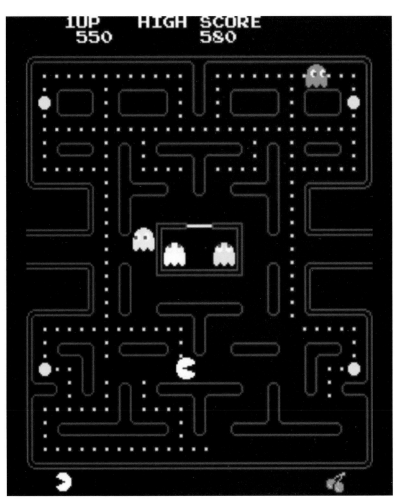

Pac-Man: consuming all before him

culture, and one that spends most of his time eating his way to success, but also he is the product of a meal. For Stephen Poole (2000), Pac-Man's insatiability makes him the very epitome of late capitalism.

Although the name of Pac-Man will be known to most, that of Billie Mitchell will be much less familiar while the significance of the number 3,333,360 is likely understood by only the most dedicated of *Pac-Man* aficionados. In theory, *Pac-Man* should be a game with an 'infinite' structure (see Newman, 2004). That is, there is no winning state, per se, no conclusion or ending from which the player emerges victorious. Instead, and in keeping with many games of this era (such as *Space Invaders* and *Asteroids*), it offers the player more and more mazes to navigate until death or tedium end the session. The machine will always win and Pac-Man will always be consumed by the ghosts that chase him. However, in practice, a bug in the game's program means that the 256th maze is corrupted, barring further progress. Rendering the game unintentionally finite, this glitch has thrown down a gauntlet to expert players who seek to perform the 'perfect' game. Gobbling down every dot and bonus piece of fruit from each of the 255 mazes earns a maximum 3,333,360 points. In 1999, Billie Mitchell became the first player to rack up a perfect score, taking five and half hours to beat the game without losing a life.[36] Undeterred, subsequent players have shifted their focus to beating Mitchell's time. Currently, Twin Galaxies, the official electronic scoreboard for videogames and pinball, lists Chris Ayra's three hours forty-two minutes and four seconds as the fastest.[37]

35. Recently re-released to celebrate *Pac-Man*'s twenty-fifth birthday, a CD is available at <www.bucknergarcia.com>.

36. See <www.mameworld.net/pacman/mitchell/mitchell.htm>.

37. See <www.twingalaxies.com>.

Publisher: Midway; **Platform**: Coin-Op.

Parachute (PR-21)
1981
Nintendo

Before GameBoy and DS, Nintendo cut its teeth in the handheld videogames marketplace with its Game & Watch series. The decision to include and market the systems as part game part timepiece is a curious one and one could be forgiven for thinking that Nintendo suffered a last-minute loss of confidence in the ability to sell a system that was just for gameplay.[38] Where later portable console systems would use interchangeable cartridges to lend them longevity, allowing them to be reinvented and reinvigorated with new software, and keep pace with changing fashions, G&W titles were hardwired to a single game. Moreover, they were simple games. Really simple. We have perhaps forgotten quite how exciting and even revolutionary the idea of handheld gaming, indeed of computers in general, was in 1980 when the first G&W titles were released, and are in danger of underestimating how impossibly futuristic it was to be able to interact with virtual worlds. Today, even 'simple' mobile phone games are usually immeasurably more complex than G&W titles like *Ball* (AC-01, 1980) or *Snoopy Tennis* (SP-30, 1982) yet we must be careful not to confuse 'simple' and 'basic', and should certainly not infer that these games are not (still) enjoyable to play. In fact, part of the pleasure of G&W games comes from the extraordinary economy of their structures and interface. Everything that is required to play the game is here, but not a thing more (except perhaps an alarm clock).

Parachute is a paean to simplicity and economy. You take on the role of a man in a rowing boat and are challenged with the task of rescuing the titular parachutists who jump from a twin-propped helicopter that hovers at the top right of the screen. The boat can move to one of three positions on screen – middle, left and right (and for 'move', do not assume that animation or scrolling is involved – instead read 'move' as a jump between one of three static positions). Conveniently, the parachutists fall along one of three trajectories, landing in the middle, left or right of the screen. Manoeuvre the boat to the right position and the skydiver will fall into your lap and be saved.

Fail to do so, and they will fall into the water and be chased by a shark that, judging by the grin it sports after a 'miss', savours your ineptitude. Miss three parachutists and the game is over. Succeed in your rescue mission and the game can, in theory at least, last forever. No variation, no added complexity, no additional trajectories, just faster and faster and faster. If variation is what you seek, the G&W's 'Game B' mode adds complication by ensuring that, at random intervals, a parachutist will become entangled in a palm tree. As you attend to his still falling comrades, he swings back and forth until falling unpredictably towards the shark's teeth.

Either side of the self-proclaimed 'widescreen' LCD that dominates *Parachute*'s casing, the player is offered just two buttons: left and right. Simple and uncomplicated. Like all G&W titles, *Parachute* has clearly been designed within the technological constraints of the early 1980s and at no point does the player feel what has subsequently become the all-too-frequent sensation that the game's ambition has been curtailed by hardware, software or time constraints. As the series matured, new features such as dual screens and directional pads were added to games such as *Donkey Kong* (DK-52, 1982), but the fundamental purity of the distilled gameplay remained constant.

The legacy of G&W is considerable. Not only are the original devices highly collectible (along with the many contemporary re-badged, bootlegged and promotional versions), but many of the design decisions continue to influence Nintendo today. The orientation and aspect of the 'widescreen' recurs in GameBoy Advance and micro, while the Dual Screen G&W series are the clear progenitors of the DS. Nintendo released a number of G&W titles, including *Parachute*, in the G&W Gallery series for GameBoy. As such, these games are now playable on the very system that brought the G&W product line to an end in 1989.

38. Tho ugh the Game & Watch moniker was used throughout the life of the series and the handhelds continued to offer the same features, the proud 'with alarm function' boast that graced early packaging soon disappeared.

Publisher: CGL; **Platform**: Game & Watch.

PaRappa the Rapper
1996
Sony Computer Entertainment Interactive

Although the term was not used at the time, *PaRappa the Rapper* is a 'rhythm action game' that sees the player adopting the role of a young dog (PaRappa) determined to win the affections of his would-be belle Sunny Funny (an irrepressibly cheery sunflower bedecked in a stripey dress and permanent smile). Skipping quickly over the impossibility of such a pairing, we find that PaRappa has discerned that the best course of action is to woo Sunny with his rapping skills and so the game begins. On the face of it, the game is simply a version of the venerable children's toy *Simon* only with the flashing lights replaced with PlayStation controller icons. However, where *Simon* requires the player to remember and recall only the sequence of lights with no regard to timing or tempo, *PaRappa the Rapper* introduces a greater degree of musicality to the performance. The game is not simply played out to a background soundtrack but, as is now commonplace in 'rhythm action' or 'beatmania' games, the music paces and structures the game. Here, then, we must ensure that PaRappa's rhymes are not only note but beat perfect. The game works by breaking down PaRappa's vocal performance into chunks that are mapped to key sequences. As a disembodied PaRappa head moves across a musical timeline at the top of the screen, controller icons appear, and pressing the corresponding buttons on the joypad triggers the next snippet of audio. Time it well and the performance is perfect. Too early or too late and, in case your ears are not sufficient to judge, on screen ratings reassure you that you are doing badly – in the nicest possible way, of course. And everybody is still smiling even after the poorest of shows.

The game is broken into a number of stages that are loosely connected by a narrative as paper-thin as the 2D graphics in the game. Each stage sees PaRappa under the tutelage of a different master who guides him through a new rap. Starting with Chop Chop Master Onion of the Fruites dojo, and moving through Prince Fleaswallow with his laid-back skank, and Inspector Mooselini the driving instructor, among others,

PaRappa's performance is ranked and rated. Following the instructions of the masters will yield success, but to attain the highest rating, 'U Rappin Cool', PaRappa must freestyle around the tunes, hitting the preset markers in time but adding his own flourishes. By moving away from a simple memory test and adding the ability to play with the tunes, and personalise the performances, the game's replay value is greatly enhanced.

That *PaRappa the Rapper* is no *Final Fantasy* or *Metal Gear Solid* in the complexity of its story or depth of its characters is of no importance. This is a game of music and performance and each stage is little more than a device to introduce a new tune to master. Indeed, once we start rapping, we enter an *8 Mile*-like state and lose ourselves in the music where all thoughts of the bizarre narrative arc or character motivations disappear as we become insistent on not letting the opportunity that comes once in a lifetime pass . . .

We should note that while he may share a similar determination to own the mic, and PaRappa may indeed proclaim to be a 'Hip Hop Hero' in the game's subtitle, he is no Eminem. Indeed, this little pup is about as far from Snoop as you can imagine. PaRappa's is a world of hand-drawn, bold, primary colours and, above all, joy. Where rap has become a staple part of the gritty, urban landscapes of games like *50 Cent Bulletproof*, PaRappa's tunes perfectly underpin its cheery, witty aesthetic. In fact, while it is the music that is ultimately its centrepiece, much of PaRappa's undeniable charm comes from its visual design and the work of lauded graphic designer Rodney Greenblat.

As the rhythm action genre gained popularity, *PaRappa the Rapper* turned from cult hit into mainstream franchise, spawning a sequel and spin-off. *PaRappa the Rapper 2* (PlayStation 2) follows a similar pattern to the original title, while *Um Jammer Lammy* charts the trials of a guitar-playing lamb who uses music to overcome her personal issues and insecurities, as you would expect.

Publisher: Sony Computer Entertainment Europe; **Platform**: Sony PlayStation.

Peter Jackson's King Kong:
The official game of the movie
2005
Ubisoft

The world of the licensed-product game remains an area of deep suspicion for the gaming audience. The franchise tie-in has given gamers a few true gems (*Star Wars*, *Spider-Man 2*) but a vastly larger number of poor cash-ins (*E.T.*, *Superman 64*). This has always been the area where the videogames establishment becomes most insecure, most unsure – almost apologetic about what it is. Strangely, whenever the games world moves in proximity to Hollywood, it transforms into a fawning ingénue of its former self. Movies appear to represent everything that games wish they were, the ultimate aspirations of the industry being often cited as 'interactive cinema'.

The announcement of the *King Kong* project was at pains to stress that this was a new kind of collaboration between these media. This was not an adaptation, but a fusion. Peter Jackson himself, fresh from the stellar success of the *Lord of the Rings* trilogy, would be having direct input into the game. As the PR put it, 'In the *King Kong* game, players will be able to experience all the power, drama and emotion of the film thanks to the interactive possibilities provided by the game.'[39] It's unclear exactly what this means, but it's obviously very exciting.

King Kong is a beautiful game, and it knows it. Spending 90 per cent of its game narrative within the confines of the tropical Skull Island it takes great care to foreground the skill with which its jungle locations are rendered. From the very outset, *Kong* forces you into a delicate balance between playing and spectating, serving to effectively draw attention to the fact that you are not just a character in a story, but a character in a story from a high-profile AAA movie blockbuster. The detail and quality with which the locations have been created generate a palpable sense of presence, indeed the phrase 'rollercoaster ride' has seldom been more apposite. The dense foliage, delicate lighting, beautifully rendered water and tasteful sonic design render the rails you are travelling along almost invisible. The pleasure is in submission to that.

If you allow it, *Kong* is about exhilaration and sensation. It will make you feel exhilarating power and skill, while making very few demands on your actual abilities as a player. Designer Michel Ancel and his team have a precise grasp of the visual language of contemporary action cinema. The action, your action, will suddenly slow for a few seconds as Kong makes a particularly impressive leap into the air, the camera will swing down in front of your avatar as they run towards you away from their pursuers. *Kong* is at pains to demonstrate its understanding not just of the source narrative but of the detailed visual style of the Hollywood blockbuster.

Perhaps the most interesting element of the game is the final section as Kong runs amok in New York. It is here that the rails the game has been propelling us along come fully into view; in fact, we are able to see them running all the way to the top of the Empire State Building. It is there, and only there, that the journey can end. The limits of interactivity are exposed, the tensions between game and source narrative come to the fore as Kong is killed by gunfire multiple times while attempting to reach the Empire State Building – in order to climb to his certain death. The rules of *King Kong* state that he must die in his fall from the building, the rules of this game allow him to die multiple times in his attempts to get to his defined place of death. To die in the street is to suffer the dreaded 'Game Over' message – but to die having fallen from the peak of the Empire State Building results in a message of congratulations.

39. Serge Hascoet, Executive Director, Worldwide Content Strategy for Ubisoft. UBIsoft PR, 12 October 2004.

Publisher: Ubisoft; **Platform**: Sony PlayStation 2, Microsoft Xbox, Nintendo GameCube, PC, Sony PlayStation Portable, Nintendo DS.

Pokémon (*Blue* and *Red*)
1996 (Japan); 1998 (US); 1999 (Europe)
Game Freak

It would be easy to dismiss *Pokémon* as a fad and consign it to the back of the cupboard with the clackers, space hopper and skateboard and while, in Europe at least, it may have passed the peak of its mainstream popularity, the franchise remains alive and well with new titles in development. Indeed, in the ten years since Pikachu and his first 150 friends were released into the world, they have become one of the largest grossing videogame series with sales topping $15 billion from a total of 150 million games sold. Along with *Super Mario* and the *Legend of Zelda* series, *Pokémon* is one of Nintendo's most valuable videogame franchises.

   Beginning life in Japan in 1996, *Pocket Monsters* became *Pokémon* only when making the leap to the US and Europe to distinguish the new games from a line of Matchbox 'Monster in my Pocket' figures. The first *Pokémon* videogames were released for the GameBoy with *Pokémon Red* and *Pokémon Blue* (originally *Red* and *Green* in Japan) providing the first introduction to the army of critters waiting to win the hearts, minds and wallets of the gaming public. The games place the player in the role of a pokémon trainer whose task is to locate and capture the wild pokémon that live in a variety of habitats in the gameworld. Captured monsters are loyal to their trainer and can be made to fight one another so as to develop their skills and abilities and propel their keeper up the league table towards becoming a poké master. Although commanding animals to fight may seem the twenty-first-century equivalent of cock fighting, there is a strong bond of friendship between trainer and his pokémon and the game promotes nurturing and environmental awareness throughout its narrative. The battles, too, are not tests of strength per se, but of strategy and technique with the objective to consider best how to deal with an opponent's roster of pokémon given the resources to hand rather than simply to destroy them. Each individually named and numbered pokémon has a different set of abilities, strengths and weaknesses, attacks and defences, depending on its species, maturity and experience level. As such, players must select a line-up of pokémon carefully, considering their resistance and vulnerability in light of the capabilities of the opponents, before sending them into battle so as to avoid losing out to rival trainers. In fact, pokémon do not die in battle but instead faint and are returned to full strength after resting.

While battling is a staple mechanic of the game and is the means of building the experience of pokémon and evolving them into stronger, more capable combatants, longevity comes from pokémon collecting. The game's tagline 'Gotta Catch 'Em All' succinctly summarises the completeism that is encouraged during play. Locating and capturing all

Pokémon: gotta catch 'em all

151 of the original 'Blue and Red' pokémon is not merely a challenge that involves patience, skill and a degree of luck, but may even be a literal impossibility for some players. Not only was the 151st pokémon 'Mew' only available to download at Nintendo promotional events and thereby not unlockable in the game without cheating, but not all of the remaining 150 can be found in either the *Blue* or *Red* versions. Instead, they are spread across the two titles and players wanting to collect the full set were required to barter and trade with a willing friend with the other variety of game or buy both cartridges themselves. While some may note the promotion of business and negotiation skills, sociality and collaboration, not surprisingly, there has been criticism of this decision that is seen by some as a cynical attempt to part children from their money (see Buckingham and Sefton-Green, 2003). The addition of new pokémon in each subsequent game has continued this trend of building consumption into the fabric of the game's completeist aesthetic. However, in light of the multimedia marketing machine that rolled into action to exploit *Pokémon* in every conceivable way from movie and TV tie-ins to clothing, card-trading games, plush toys and figures, collecting 'em all has long since meant more than buying videogames. It seems hard to believe that beneath Pikachu's beaming, yellow visage beats the heart of a ruthless businessman but he must have been paying attention to all those trainers doing their poké-deals.

Publisher: Nintendo; **Platform**: Nintendo GameBoy.

Pong
1972
Atari

There is a common misconception among fans and scholars of videogames that places *Pong* as the first videogame and, while debate rages as to whether Willy Higginbotham's *Tennis for Two* (1958) or Steve Russell's *Spacewar* (1962) deserves the accolade depending on how we define 'videogame', we can be certain that *Pong* came at least ten years too late to qualify.[40] Indeed, *Pong* was not even the first game that its creator Nolan Bushnell had developed and a year earlier *Computer Space* was released to a distinctly cool public who were put off by the complexity of the control system with its myriad buttons. For a generation of players used to one-armed-bandits and pinball machines, *Computer Space* was simply too involved, demanding too much investment and little short-term thrill. While the commercial failure of *Computer Space* may have deterred others, Bushnell used it as a learning experience and *Pong* was designed with simplicity and immediacy in mind.

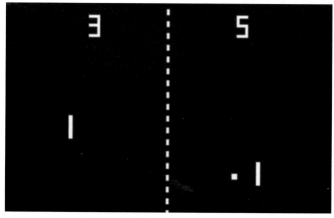

Pong: avoid missing ball for high score

Most obviously, *Pong* replaced *Computer Space*'s esoteric, science-fiction abstraction space battles, gravitational pull and black holes with a pared-down simulation of an already-known activity – table tennis. It placed on the screen only the barest of information required for the game to function, and so players were greeted with just a ball, two bats and a running score. The hardware interface moved from *Computer Space*'s confusing mess of multiple buttons and switches to just two controllers, one for each player, and so hardware and software were immediately linked in an effective and uncomplicated manner. The controller on the left moved the bat on the left, while the right-hand controller operated the right-hand bat. All of this added up to an intuitive, approachable game that required none of the explanation or interpretation that had blighted Bushnell's previous title. *Pong*'s famously brief, almost curt, instructions speak of the turnaround in the design that occurred in the year after *Computer Space*'s failure. 'Avoid missing ball for high score' paved the way for future arcade games that would continue to trade on intuitiveness, simplicity and instant gratification, while its curiously negative assertion perfectly captured the frustration and compulsion of play and hinted at the benefit of repetition and practice.

In truth, much of *Pong*'s simplicity and economy was as much a consequence of technological limitation as any Zen-like search for gameplay and representational purity. Early 1970s graphics processors were simply incapable of rendering a circular ball and so *Pong*'s 'ball' is square. In its functional world of wholly symbolic forms, this poses no threat to the verisimilitude of the virtual table-tennis experience, however, and certainly did not dampen players' voracious appetites for the game. Home conversions capitalising on the game's popularity were plentiful in the 1970s, with Atari's official conversion joined by a plethora of imitators and clones. Subsequently, the scalability and adaptability of *Pong*'s essential game mechanics have kept it alive with updated versions, such as *Pong – The Next Level*, for PlayStation, that change graphics and even move away from the ping-pong theme to football or ice hockey. Meanwhile, the comparatively modest technical demands of the game have made it an ideal candidate for conversion to mobile platforms.[41] Over thirty years on, *Pong* is still being discovered by new players but, perhaps most importantly, its legacy is felt in every arcade game that invites its players into parting with their coins by promising immediate fun without the obfuscation of instructions.

40. See Kent (2001) for more on the early history of videogames.
41. See Salen and Zimmerman (2003) on *Pong*'s enduring design.

Publisher: Atari; **Platform**: Coin-Op.

Porrasturvat (Stair Dismount)
2002
Jetro Lauha

One of the definitive water-cooler games, *Porrasturvat* – or *Stair Dismount* – became one of the best-loved downloads of the Slashdot set. Created by Finnish developer Jetro Lauha from demo group tAAt, it has achieved legendary status for the purity of its concept and style of execution.

Porrasturvat comes with a remarkably uncomplicated premise. A 3D rendering of a man stands at the top of a flight of stairs. There is no contextual graphical material (not even a banister or hand rail), no sense of this staircase existing in any particular space or time, no narrative that explains how the man came to be at the top of a flight of stairs that lead to and from nowhere. Hugely abstract, although beautiful in its simplicity, its starkly sharp-edged, shiny-surfaced, untextured, single light-sourced aesthetic harks back to Disney's *Tron* (1982) and the groundbreaking computer graphic experiments of the 1960s.

The object of the exercise is, unsurprisingly enough, to get the man from the top to the bottom of the stairs. This may seem like the least imaginative, and certainly least expansive, platform game ever devised. Where Nintendo's seminal *Super Mario World* boasted ninety-six levels of treacherous, imaginative labyrinths, *Porrasturvat* gives the player just a single flight of steps. And how should we direct the player to the bottom of the stairs? As quickly as possible, perhaps? That would certainly fit with the aesthetic of videogames. But *Porrasturvat* is not concerned with time or at least only insofar as time and space are inexorably linked. *Porrasturvat* is a game about physics, about inertia and gravity, about the complex ways in which forces react, interact and combine with one another. If all this sounds a little dry and rather too reminiscent of a school lesson in which every force is met with an equal and opposite then fret not because *Porrasturvat* is also about people falling over and the impossibly funny sights and sounds that accompany a truly spectacular descent.

Unusually, in *Porrasturvat* the player does not control the man on the stairs directly. Rather, the player exerts control over a force acting upon the man, a force whose direction and strength are variable and that may be used to virtually prod the protagonist who then, dutifully obeying the laws of physics, falls step by step from top to bottom of this flight of steps that begins to look more and more like an instrument of torture as the game progresses. Choosing a point of the body, perhaps the left calf or right elbow, the player exerts the force by clicking on the courteously named 'Dismount' button, whereupon the computer-generated rag-doll man's leg or arm is summarily whipped away. The force of the blow obviously sends the poor chap toppling downward and, if he is really unlucky and the player's fortune holds, he will hit every step on the way down, limbs twisting and contorting beneath him as he goes, all represented with elegant and subtle animation that gives the torso weight and mass. And

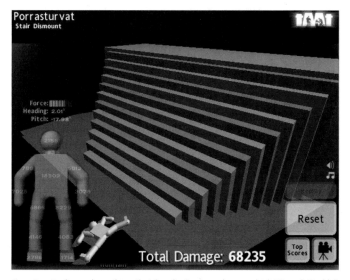

Porrasturvat: who can honestly say that they don't enjoy seeing somebody trip and stumble?

so, what begins as a seemingly dreary exercise in physics very soon descends into a potentially brutal bloodbath of graphic aggression and violence. What stops this being just plain nasty, however, are the sound effects. Was each contact with cold, hard stair accompanied by a bone-crunching effect then the game may well be a sickening experience, but as each trip, stumble and bump sees the hapless CG man emit a frankly comic exclamation, the overall effect is one of farce. The resulting string of 'ooh-ahh-ow' is as understated and genteel as the 'dismount' name itself.

The game takes the player's voyeurism and enables it to truly enjoy itself in all three dimensions. tAAt give us action replays (complete with flashing 'r' in the top corner) and a variety of camera angles to choose from. As well as simply giving us a licence to enjoy the doll's pain, it offers us a complete tool-set with which to dole out, observe and re-observe our own sadism. This is, of course, is very funny.

Who would have thought that the most notable and interesting thing about a game whose sole purpose is to push a man down a flight of stairs without motivation would be reservation, restraint and understatement? *Porrasturvat* is certainly puerile, yet its childishness is handled with a maturity that makes it a rare and genuinely funny experience. Call it Schadenfreude, if you need to rationalise it, but who can honestly say that they don't enjoy seeing somebody trip and stumble? Certainly, the game has won a place in the hearts of information workers the world over who shell out of their desktops at lunchtime to spend some time torturing the helpless.

Stair Dismount was so well received that it was followed by a sequel, *Truck Dismount*. Similar in premise, this developed the concept by placing the same rag doll in opposition to a large truck. Hilarity ensues. Most recently, tAAt have begun development on *Dismount Levels*, an editor that will allow users to create their own levels for the game. In this way, the public may use their own creativity to develop new paradigms of cruelty to anonymous grey puppets.

Publisher: tAAt; **Platform**: Windows, Mac OS X, Linux.

Puzzle Bobble
1994
Taito

Inexplicably retitled *Bust-a-Move* outside Japan, and released in 1994, *Puzzle Bobble* seems to be a game out of its time. Audiovisually, it is simple almost to the point of being Spartan, and harks back to earlier decades of uncomplicated game design and representation. Mixing elements from Sega's multicoloured gem-matching *Columns* (which, in itself, owes no small debt to *Tetris*), Taito's own *Space Invaders* and Milton Bradley's (non-video) game *Connect 4*, it is a remarkably simple, abstract puzzle game. Like many games of the 1970s and 1980s, the game takes place in a confined play area bounded by a single screen with no scrolling and, in a similar fashion to *Tetris*, revolves around trying to keep the play area free from the debris that incessantly, and inexplicably, insists on appearing and ruining the perfect emptiness. Where *Tetris* hurls a never-ending succession of tetraminoes at the player and privileges geometry and symmetry in demanding the player translate and rotate the various block configurations to make the most efficient arrangement, *Puzzle Bobble* takes a different tack. Here, rotating and flipping is unnecessary as there is but one type of object to deal with – the ball – and as a sphere there is little to be gained from rotating it. Instead, *Puzzle Bobble* creates variation through colour. *Tetris* was to all intents and purposes a monochrome game as its success on the GameBoy serves to illustrate, and where colour was used in conversions it played no significant role other than to beautify proceedings. In *Puzzle Bobble*, however, play is centred around colour. A number of multicoloured balls populate the play area at the start of each game and the player's simple and sole task is to stop their accumulation. Unfortunately, the player's only weapon against the coloured balls is a cannon that fires . . . more coloured balls. As a strategy for ridding the world of coloured balls, this seems a poor one that is doomed to failure. Luckily, it is one of the time-honoured traditions of puzzle videogames that a certain number of like-coloured objects in close proximity to one another will disappear. Phew. In the case of *Puzzle Bobble*, matching

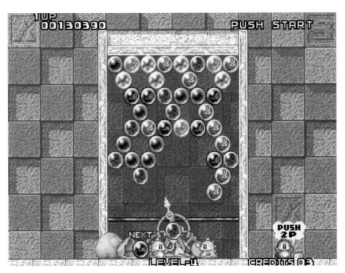

Puzzle Bobble: Bub and Bob sweat nervously as the screen becomes dangerously full of balls

three balls of the same colour will see them vanish. The game, then, develops *Space Invaders*' mechanic in placing the player at the foot of the play area, giving them fairly limited freedom of movement, and tasking them with defeating the onslaught of a foe that descends inexorably from above.

Just like *Tetris* and *Space Invaders*, the visible markers of success are only fleetingly seen in *Puzzle Bobble* as a series of like-coloured balloons disappear in a puff of smoke, and what remains on screen is a palpable reminder of failure, of what could not be cleared. More than that, the detritus is mostly of the player's own making. It was they, after all, that fired the majority of those balls from their cannon. Had they been more skilful or thoughtful, then this mess could look so different. The state of the play area is the most effective feedback mechanism in *Puzzle Bobble* and serves as a constantly updated indicator of progress and prowess, albeit in the most negative manner. Consequently, and perhaps perversely, for a medium so often characterised in terms of visual excess and multisensory bombardment, the object of *Puzzle Bobble,* like that of many puzzle games, such as *Lumines* and *Meteos*, is to rid the screen of material and to return it to its pristine, blank neutrality.

The controls of the cannon are extremely simple. It can be angled left and right and can fire balls from the bottom to the top of the screen, thereby requiring just three buttons, making the game supremely adaptable to a variety of hardware interfaces including those like mobile phones not primarily designed for gaming. Indeed, after first appearing in the arcades and subsequently being converted to almost every computer, console and handheld platform, in 2005 the game was released for mobile phones in the shape of *Puzzle Bobble Mobile*. Besides its infuriatingly simple and compelling gameplay, and excellent two-player mode in which players battle head-to-head filling their opponent's play area with their debris cleared from their own screen, *Puzzle Bobble*'s enduring success can be attributed to two factors. First, while the game could easily be presented in a wholly abstract way like *Columns* and *Tetris*, Taito injected considerable personality by resurrecting two characters from their back-catalogue. Bub and Bob, the dinosaurs first seen in *Bubble Bobble*, are placed in charge of the cannon and their charmingly naive animations, sweating nervously as the screen becomes dangerously full of balls and jumping head over heels after a large clearance, lend the proceedings humour, individuality and charm. Second, Taito's designers have managed to sustain a large number of sequels that keep the franchise alive and vital by taking seemingly minor twists and tweaks and allowing them to exert enormous effect upon the gameplay. As such, while the ability to bounce balls off the ceiling of the play area, or the introduction of different sizes of balls might sound almost trivially insignificant, their impact on the game is immeasurably large and creates a qualitatively different play experience that demands new tactics and delivers new pleasures.

Publisher: Taito; **Platform**: Coin-Op (Neo-Geo).

Radiant Silvergun
1998
Treasure

Since its release in 1998, *Radiant Silvergun* has attained almost mythical status. For a game that belongs to a comparatively unpopular genre (the 'shoot-em-up'), that was only converted for the comparatively unsuccessful Sega Saturn home console (comprehensively trounced in the marketplace by Sony's PlayStation), that was never released outside Japan, and that is so fiendishly complex that it is practically unplayable to most players, this is not bad going. This last point is of no real importance to most players, though, as they are unlikely to ever be granted the opportunity to play the game. Nonetheless, *Radiant Silvergun* is remarkably well known and revered and, through a combination of its relative rarity and extreme difficulty, has become an unofficial poster-child of the hardcore gamer. Second-hand copies change hands through specialist games dealers and on eBay with three-figure price tags.

However, although it would be easy to write off *Radiant Silvergun* as a fanatic's curio, it is important to note that the game's reputation is well deserved. While the limited release and resulting obscurity of the title certainly contribute an air of mystique and give owners and cognoscenti alike a feeling of exclusivity and subcultural kinship, the game is a true masterpiece. It is by no means the first vertically scrolling shooter, but it perfectly marries inventive level design, sumptuous audiovisual representation, excess and restraint, the visceral thrill of destruction, and the contemplation and thoughtfulness of puzzling and strategic planning. However, on first glance, the game appears almost unfathomably complex. Placed at the controls of a solitary spaceship flying inexorably 'up' the screen, the player is literally bombarded by wave upon wave of enemy craft and missiles from the very outset. The sheer number of objects on screen – all intent on the player's destruction – is as initially bewildering as it is technically impressive given that the

Sega Saturn console was derided for its apparent lack of graphical and general processing horsepower. Fortunately, while the player might be ludicrously outnumbered, their ship is bristling with weapons systems. In fact, a total of seven weapons are available, each with their own speciality and weakness, all of which are required at different points in the game to tackle specific challenges. Unusually, all weapons are usable from the start of the game and, in this way, *Radiant Silvergun* eschews the traditional structure of shooting games that sees a woefully underpowered ship gradually earning and acquiring additional capabilities throughout the course of the game via 'power-ups'. Instead, the player blasts off with a full arsenal of deadly ordnance, straight into the heat of battle. Indeed, such is *Radiant Silvergun*'s level of difficulty that its opening stages match those of the culmination of most other games in the genre.

Closer inspection reveals some patterns in the on screen chaos, although this serves only to further complicate the issue. Enemy ships are not all the same colour – some are red, some blue and others yellow – and destroying three of the same colour in sequence rewards the player with a hefty score bonus that grows as these 'chains' of three shots are themselves chained together to form an uninterrupted sequence of polychromatic destruction. The centrality of chaining means that indiscriminate shooting is the tactic of novices only. One of *Radiant Silvergun*'s innovations is that it encourages a far greater degree of tactical consideration than most shoot-em-ups and, perhaps perversely for a game in this genre, requires the deliberate avoidance of some enemies lest they break the chain. As such, the game introduces a strong puzzle element in requiring the player to consider and plan, as well as execute, a route through the onslaught. This is possible because the game's enemy attack patterns are predefined rather than random, meaning that they can be learned and planned for. As such, the game privileges memory, recall and strategy over 'twitch' gaming.

Such is the unforgiving nature of *Radiant Silvergun*, that it remains one of the few games that can deliberately (rather than through bugs or glitches) place the player in a position where they cannot win. Failing to sufficiently charge the ship's weapons and despatch the penultimate Boss enemy speedily enough will result in the untimely appearance of the final enemy who is invincible. There are plenty of videogames that are difficult to complete, but it is rare for a developer to create one that is, or at least can be, impossible.

Publisher: ESP; **Platform**: Coin-Op, Sega Saturn.

Resident Evil
1996
Capcom

From the earliest days, videogame dialogue has been of variable quality to say the least. While there are exceptions such as the *Half-Life* series, cringingly poor writing and unintentionally amusing translation abound with Toaplan's MegaDrive conversion of *Zero Wing* spawning the phrase 'All your base are belong to us' that has fired the imagination and taken on a cultish life of its own.[42] Thanks to the PlayStation and its CD-ROM storage bringing the possibility of live-action video sequences to videogames, the need for subtitled computer-generated graphics subsided and living, breathing actors could be filmed speaking the lines (while trying not to bump into the scenery). Through its use of live-action movie sequences, *Resident Evil* took third-rate dialogue to new depths. This is not a criticism, however. *Resident Evil* is a videogame B-movie and the hammy overacting and creaking script perfectly set the scene for the horrors to come.

Resident Evil (originally known as *Biohazard* in its Japanese release) is a 'survival horror' game and, just as that name suggests, the object of the exercise is to try and stay alive for as long as possible. As an officer of STARS (Special Tactics And Rescue Squad), the player is charged with investigating a series of murders whose trail ultimately leads to an apparently overgrown and long-since vacated mansion. Upon closer inspection, however, the team uncover a biological weapons facility operated by the evil 'Umbrella' organisation. Experimenting with viral engineering and genetic modification, Umbrella has created an army of mutant creatures ranging from humanoid zombies to vicious spiders, crows and wolves. Needless to say, all of the genetically modified denizens of the house are hell-bent on killing the players and harvesting their corpses to feed their seemingly insatiable desire for blood.

Almost as soon as the game commences, it is clear that *Resident Evil* is inspired by the *Dead Series* movies of George A. Romero both in terms of its setting, with its hordes of zombies intent on tearing the still-living flesh from anything that moves, but also in its cinematography. Though the use of a static virtual camera to display the action to the player as a series of 'rooms' to be explored is not groundbreaking in itself, *Resident Evil*'s camera placement and *mise en scène* create a game that is manifestly a homage to Romero and the zombie horror genre.

As a game, *Resident Evil* has some interesting quirks that have long exercised the attentions of fans and critics. Like *Tomb Raider*, the player cannot save their progress at will and save points are dotted around the gameworld. In *Resident Evil*, the player must locate an ink ribbon and typewriter, which certainly adds to the tension and suspense of the game and imposes its structure and tempo on play but is not particularly accommodating of those players who wish or need to break their play sessions on their own terms. The game is lent a certain realism in that zombie-killing and ridding the world of genetic mutation cannot be readily stopped for dinnertime. Chief among the points of debate over *Resident Evil*, however, is the control system and there can be little doubt that, regardless of its quality and invention, the game is not intuitive to play. The complication comes from the way in which it mixes a second- or third-person viewpoint where the player's character is seen on screen, with a set of controls and inputs more usually found in first-person viewpoint games such as *DOOM* or *Quake*. What this means in practice is that controls are not relative to the player's character but rather are 'hard wired' so, even if the on screen avatar is facing left, the player must press 'up' on their joypad to make them walk forward requiring a cognitive disconnection of the virtual space of the gameworld and the physical and bodily space of the control pad and hand. It would be easy to deride this as an example of poor-quality design but, of course, this complication is part of the game's aesthetic. Part of the pleasure of horror film comes from the way it plays with the audience's degree of control over the narrative (see Krzywinska, 2002). In *Resident Evil* things are more subtle and sophisticated, however. 'Out of control' is made most manifest and faced with a pack of wolves leaping through a window or a corpse that reveals itself to be undead and really quite intent on helping the player join them in the netherworld, they are literally rooted to the spot, unable to move no matter how hard they try and which buttons they instinctively jab at. The horror in *Resident Evil* comes not simply from the gruesome visuals or even from the atmospheric music and sound effects, though they are doubtless important ingredients. The horror in *Resident Evil* is generated partly by the interface itself. The controls do not merely mediate the action or provide a mechanism to engage with it, they *create* it. If ever a counterblast to the taken-for-granted assumption that videogame interfaces must be 'transparent' was needed (see Rollings and Morris, 2000, for example), Capcom's masterpiece is the bloodstained, but still shining, case study.

To reinforce the game's filmic lineage, among the many sequels, conversions and adaptations, is a *Director's Cut* that boasts enhanced character graphics and 'new camera angles'.[43] Interestingly, the franchise has spawned two feature films of its own. However, while Romero's services were originally employed as scriptwriter for the first film, he did not complete the project. Given the games' inspiration and suffusion in the world of cult horror film, it is something of a surprise to see the glossy, Hollywood action films that seem only marginally and tenuously connected with the games.

42. <www.newgrounds.com/collection/allyourbase.html>.
43. *Resident Evil Director's Cut* (PlayStation version) boxart (Capcom/Virgin Interactive), 1997 (outside back cover).

Publisher: Capcom; **Platform**: Sony PlayStation.

Rez
2002
United Game Artists

On one hand, *Rez* is a videogame about synthesis. On first glance, the game may even seem derivative and, superficially at least, it seems to bear more than a passing similarity to a range of other games. It takes the shooting and relentless travelling through the gameworld from Sega's earlier *Space Harrier* and *Panzer Dragoon*. It takes the player-character mechanic of *Vib Ribbon* and replaces 'lives' or a health indicator with a six-stage system of evolution. Visually, the game is equally referential and makes an explicit nod towards Disney's early computer-generated movie *Tron*, with its sharp, geometric lines. The resulting wireframe graphical environment of unshaded, unfilled polygon meshes oozes mannered retro chic and is steeped in the aesthetic and technologies of classic 1970s and 1980s games such as *Asteroids* and *Battlezone*. In itself, this combination of elements and visual styles is not particularly notable even though *Rez* pulls it off with an impeccable sense of style that flows through its outer space blasting to its menu screens and instruction manuals. Hybridisation, after all, is a staple feature of videogames development with genres and forms being continually merged and adapted to create new genres and subgenres, new devices, new game structures and designs. What is interesting about *Rez* is the way in which it attempts to create new forms of sensory experience for the player. *Rez* is not merely a game concerned with synthesis. It is a game concerned with synaesthesia. This condition describes the situation in which the stimulation of one sense triggers apparent sensory response in another. What this means in practice is that a synaesthete might see sounds or hear colours. Synaesthesia has been explored by many artists, including Wassily Kandinsky, whose early twentieth-century 'improvisations' became an explicit point of reference for the team developing *Rez*.[44] Indeed, during preproduction, the game was known as the *K-Project* and this name still lingers on in the name of the central processing unit in *Rez*.[45] As such, while it might be apparently located squarely within the cultural space of games, film and popular culture, *Rez*'s most interesting and significant influence is a French-Russian abstract painter.

In fact, *Rez*'s study of synaesthesia is particularly interesting in examining not only the melding of audio and video, music and graphics, but also tactility. The PlayStation joypad's 'Dual Shock' feature that vibrates or 'rumbles' the controller in the player's hands is used by many games and is often employed to add weight to on screen action or even warn players of upcoming dangers by acting as an alarm. In *Rez*, however, this controller function becomes a seamless part of the experiential totality of the game. By destroying the multitude of airborne computer-virus enemies, the player essentially performs a musical soundtrack that is 'released' from the controller in the form of rhythmic vibrations. In *Rez*, the PlayStation joypad is manifestly both an input and output device simultaneously. For the more adventurous, the Japanese version of *Rez* shipped with a limited edition 'Trance Vibrator' that generated an even more intense rumble effect. Describing the device, *Rez*'s producer, Tetsuya Mizuguchi, indicated the versatility of the peripheral. 'You can put it anywhere – your foot, your back, your waist . . . It's up to our customers' imagination.'[46] Some of *Rez*'s customers have seen to it that the 'Trance Vibrator' has enjoyed a second life stimulating more than just the imaginations of players.[47]

44. <www.gamasutra.com/features/20050506/hawkins_pfv.htm>.

45. <www.sonicteam.com/rez/e/story/index.html>.

46. <www.wired.com/wired/archive/11.05/play.html?pg=6>.

47. <www.gamegirladvance.com/archives/2002/10/26/sex_in_games_rezvibrator.html>.

Publisher: Sega; **Platform**: Sega Dreamcast, Sony PlayStation 2.

Ridge Racer
1993 (Coin-Op); 1994 (PlayStation)
Namco

Where *WipEout* defined the posture and potency of the PlayStation in Europe with its fast-paced gameplay and club culture infused aesthetic, in its home territory of Japan, the duty of selling Sony's console fell almost exclusively to Namco's *Ridge Racer*. In many ways, this might appear an odd choice. *WipEout* communicated the next-generation power of the PlayStation with its high-concept, futuristic aesthetic and gameplay innovation, while *Ridge Racer* was an arcade conversion of one of the oldest videogame genres – car racing. However, while players may have recently become accustomed to lazy ports of coin-operated games that cash in on their popularity without adding anything to the mix, and to powerful home consoles that are more than capable of replicating the graphics, sounds and experiences of coin-operated machines, it is important to remember that the relationship between console and arcade has not always been one of such equity.

  Throughout the 1980s and early 1990s, the arcade reigned supreme. Technologically, coin-operated cabinets were in a different league to their comparatively underpowered home console counterparts. While custom hardware interfaces such as lightguns, steering wheels, and even skis and bicycles, were the most obvious expression of this difference, graphically and sonically, too, few consoles could hold a candle to specialised coin-operated equipment. As such, the arcade set the benchmark for videogames and conversions were typically poor facsimiles of the original that may have played well on their own terms, but often had missing features and were audiovisually limited. And yet, or perhaps because of this, the desire for arcade games in the home was voracious and any number of developers and publishers were only too happy to exploit this trend. Soon, the term 'arcade perfect' would become part of every gamer's vocabulary and most would understand that it was used with varying degrees of truthfulness. With *Ridge Racer*, Namco made things difficult for other developers and turned 'arcade perfect' from rhetorical marketing spiel to a simple product description. And in doing so, it proved that nobody should underestimate the power of PlayStation, just like Sony said.

Graphically, *Ridge Racer* was peerless. The solidity of the car models, the speed of movement, the richness of the textures all seem somewhat crude to today's eyes but in 1994 that was the state of the art in arcades and to have it appearing on your television in your living room courtesy of Sony's box of tricks was a small miracle. Of course, while this was great news for console players, the picture was less rosy for arcade developers and operators. The rise of the super-powerful console and the rapid narrowing of the performance gap between home and coin-operated gaming technology began the slow and steady demise of the arcade both in terms of its technological dominance and culturally as a venue and site of social as well as computer interaction.

Perversely, as gaming tastes have changed, *Ridge Racer's* defining facet has become one of the basis of criticism of the game. As an arcade racer, *Ridge Racer's* handling and physics model have only a nodding acquaintance with reality – cars powerslide around corners at phenomenal speeds, bouncing off barriers and other cars like a pachinko ball as they go. There is no doubt that this is exhilarating and fun but it could not be further from the seriousness of the simulation aesthetic of titles like *Gran Turismo* that have gone on to become the chequered flag-wavers of PlayStation racing. However, the *Ridge Racer* brand lives on with the sixth instalment released for Xbox 360 and a updated port of the original arcade conversion completing a full lap and appearing as a launch title for PlayStation Portable.

Publisher: Namco; **Platform**: Coin-Op, Sony PlayStation.

Robotron: 2084
1982
Williams Electronics

'Remember . . . You are the last hope of mankind . . .' It's a big responsibility to bear, but it's one that frequently falls on the shoulders of the average videogamer. Utterly unforgiving, yet simplistic in its design, *Robotron: 2084* offered a sustained intensity of play that had rarely been seen in western arcades before. Essentially, *Robotron* is about sustained, overwhelming pressure.

Robotron makes strides in dictating precise strategies for creating adrenal rushes in the player. Stripped of the trappings of any particular visual flourishes – the design is functional, rather than artful – the game wears its mechanics on its sleeve. Anything that gets in the way of the core game system has been removed. While nodding towards the thin veil of a sci-fi plot in its introductory text, Robotron quickly dispenses with any particular narrative trappings. For a game that was originally conceived with no shooting in it at all (the player would lead the enemies towards their own deaths on electrodes), *Robotron* emerged from a short design process as one of the most intense shooting games in the arcades and marks a peak of Eugene Jarvis's career.

Considering the original gun-free design, Jarvis remembers, 'It was fun for about fifteen minutes . . . But pacifism has its limits. Gandhi, the video game, would have to wait; it was time for some killing action. We wired up the "fire" joystick and the chaos was unbelievable.'[48]

Robotron bombards the solitary player with waves of escalating attacks. Their single purpose in earlier levels, to move towards the player – they might be easily avoided in small numbers but, like Romero Zombies, they're much happier attacking in large groups. The sheer volume of the threat on screen itself generates a visceral excitement in *Robotron* that is hard to match. With the entire game taking place within the confines of the rectangular screen (there is no *Asteroids*-style wrap-around space here), the claustrophobia is intense.

The innovation for which *Robotron* is chiefly remembered, though, is its twin controls. To date, arcade games had generally required the protagonist to fire in the direction he was moving. Jarvis, drawing on a mechanic suggested by an earlier game, *Beserk*, in which if the player held down fire they would remain stationary and could shoot in all directions, hit upon the radical innovation of wholly separating the movement of the player from the direction of their fire. *Robotron* was played with two separate joysticks mounted on the cabinet, one to move and one to fire. This ambidextrous mechanism created a remarkably freeing sense of control. While critics have raved about this particular feature for years, it is Jarvis himself who describes it most appositely as, 'insanity at its best'.[49]

As a gaming audience prepares to step up to the next generation of platform, players have developed, become desensitised to audiovisual spectacle. The leap from PlayStation to PlayStation 2 to PlayStation 3 is visible, but nonetheless something we can foresee to a large extent. Imagine in the late 1970s . . . 'They were totally awesome. To go from a blank screen to "Pong" to something like "Space Invaders" was mind-blowing.'[50]

48. <www.dadgum.com/halcyon/BOOK/JARVIS.HTM>.

49. Ibid.

50. Ibid

Publisher: Williams Electronics; **Platform**: Coin-Op.

The Secret of Monkey Island
1990
LucasArts

When the shortlists of 'funny games' are compiled, *Monkey Island* and its LucasArts adventure stable mates such as *Day of the Tentacle* and *Full Throttle* are always included. Over a period of five years, a small team developed some of the best-loved adventure titles of all time around their unique game engine, entitled SCUMM. The point-and-click adventure genre is synonymous with these games, which set both the system and the standard for many years to follow.

As well as pioneering a new kind of interaction system, arguably these games also represented the transition point between the text-adventures of old and the move to wholly eliminating the written word from the game. The SCUMM games represent some of the best, and sadly last, examples of literacy and written-wit in videogaming.

SCUMM games are about narrative wit. They clearly loved story, they were driven by it and they (most importantly) subverted it. Wearing their 'gameness' on their sleeve, bringing postmodernism to low-brow pop culture long before Kevin Williamson did so with *Scream*, they made the player feel smart just for playing. Jokes included a sequence in which the player was asked to insert disks #98, #27 and #36 (despite the game itself being supplied on only eight), characters from previous LucasArts titles appearing to plug their games and a particularly audacious 'insult swordfight' (nodding to *Cyrano De Bergerac*) with insults composed by noted science-fiction author Orson Scott-Card.

The *Monkey Island* games (there were three more sequels) were all also unmoving in their refusal to allow the player to die. The authors expressed a frustration with previous text-adventures in which the player could be instantly killed simply by entering a room, with no warning that death might be the outcome. Indeed, the only means to die in *Monkey Island* occurs if the player chooses to leave their protagonist underwater for more than ten minutes (having boasted earlier than he can hold his breath for ten minutes).

Working within the considerable confines of the early PC and Amiga platforms, SCUMM games understood that 'cinematic' gameplay was in no way contingent on photo-realism in graphics. 'Cinematic' is about rhythm, about editing, about scale and (importantly) about referencing genre archetypes (the *Half-Life* series from Valve equally displays this perspective). At time of writing, Stephen Spielberg and Electronic Arts are teaming up to create 'emotional gameplay' now that the 'technology is ready to deliver photo-real experiences'. Photo-realism is an expensive red herring. SCUMM achieved cinematic gameplay within a wholly 2D game engine.

As the adventure genre fell out of commercial favour, many of the original SCUMM developers went on to work on other notable titles and projects. In particular, Tim Schaefer created the fine *Psychonauts*, Noah Falstein became a games theorist and serious games advocate, Hal Barwood continued to develop titles at LucasArts and Ron Gilbert blogs his bitterness at grumpygamer.com

Publisher: LucasArts; **Platform**: MS-DOS, Atari ST, Macintosh, Commodore Amiga.

The Sentinel
1986
Geoff Crammond

Once again, the humble BBC would prove to be the original platform for a genre-shatteringly original title. Like *Elite* before it, the title wouldn't remain on the BBC for long – also like *Elite*, this was a game that made no effort to hide its cerebral nature, while still maintaining an entirely time-driven adrenalin rush.

The single eye that gazed out from the cover signified a great deal about the core concept of this unusual title. Essentially a game about transference, it shares similarities in this thematic sense with *Paradroid*, but is a far more complex beast to play. Upon reading the instructions for the game, one could be forgiven for being less than excited. The action concerns an attempt by the player to take over the all-seeing Sentinel, who stands, rotating slowly – at the highest point on the landscape. The esoteric instruction and inflated sci-fi context feel impenetrable, but the game itself proves simple to understand once underway. Like the best games, however, it rapidly becomes incredibly difficult to master. Like *Elite* with its countless galaxies for exploration, Crammond too chose not to skimp on the challenge and supplied the player with some 10,000 levels to conquer.

The virtually unanimously euphoric reviews at the time focused on this being the 'clever' game for home computers. It was co-opted to demonstrate to all naysayers that the computer *could* be a platform for intelligent play after all. But while the consumer press at the time alluded to this being comparable to chess in its ludic purity, *The Sentinel* is very much a computer game. While drawing on a grand tradition of board games (most visibly in its use of a chequered base-landscape), it leans heavily on creating urgency through the emerging language of the computer game. Beginning slowly, the higher the player proceeds up the landscape, the more visible they become to the slowly rotating Sentinel. All strategising on the part of the player must take place during the time it takes for the Sentinel to revolve, for if they can be seen, they can be attacked.

The game's visual design also deserves note. As one of the first games to render solid 3D shapes, it hinted at the kind of immersion that virtual reality was apparently going to deliver. Even though this was rendered incredibly slowly, the delay didn't deter lovers of the game. Indeed, the pace seemed to add to the hypnotic, surreal beauty of it. *The Sentinel* is remembered both as a fusion of ages of gaming, as a demonstration of the creativity of computer games – and most particularly as another marker of a point in time where it seemed anything was permissible. While nostalgia hasn't been kind to many of the mid-1980s titles, *The Sentinel* stands the test of time by purely and simply wearing its gameplay on its sleeve. As one reviewer in *Zzap!64* magazine presciently put it, 'It's all game.'[51]

51. <www.zzap64.co.uk/zzap20/senti.html>.

Publisher: Firebird; **Platform**: BBC Micro.

Shadow of the Colossus
2005 (Japan, US); 2006 (Europe)
Sony Computer Entertainment Inc.

Developed by the same team that brought the exquisite understatement of *Ico* to the PlayStation 2, it is unsurprising to note that *Shadow of the Colossus* is a game that bears many similar traits. Visually, the desaturated graphics return and not only speak of an artistry and sensibility that continues to find inspiration outside of the worlds and histories of videogames but that also lend an otherworldly quality to the action. Yet, as with *Ico*, this otherworldliness creates no detachment or distance between player and character. Rather, the game's aesthetic, replete with its streaming sunlight and hazy coronas, creates the impression of a half-remembered episode relived and recounted through the mists of time. Chief among the similarities between the two games, however, is the scale of the gameworld. In *Ico*, it is the castle in which the majority of the game is played out that literally dwarfs the player and creates the sense of being lost and helpless. *Shadow of the Colossus* takes a rather different approach in which the very land itself wakes from its slumber and becomes the player's nemesis. But this is no platform game where the arrangement of the environment creates a virtual obstacle course. In *Shadow of the Colossus*, huge, living creatures comprised of stone and earth, which seem both organic and inorganic simultaneously, roam the world and must be destroyed in order to bring back to life an unnamed girl whose destiny the player has become responsible for. The titular colossi are building-sized and tower above the player's character and trusty steed. Such is their immensity that they cannot simply be attacked from the ground but must be climbed in order that the player reach the inevitable weakspots that will send them crashing, lifeless, to earth. As each colossus requires a different technique to defeat it, much of the game is spent mountaineering, planning and testing routes up these giant creatures.

In presenting an experience that eschews the normal action of a videogame and centres solely on the epic battles that would usually

Shadow of the Colossus: unwittingly evil

come at the ends of levels or stages, *Shadow of the Colossus* distils the videogame form to such an extent that one might be forgiven for thinking that it simply panders to those players in search of instant gratification, excess and the bombardment of the senses that comes from each spectacular skirmish. However, what is most striking about the game is the emotional intensity of the experience. There is a real sense of connection with the world, a presence in the shoes of 'Wander' the protagonist, and a genuine feeling of longing and yearning for the lost girl. But, this is no simple binary tale of black and white, good and evil. There is ambiguity and complexity in the emotional landscape of *Shadow of the Colossus* and, unusually, for a videogame, the language extends beyond happiness and sadness, right and wrong, to encompass feelings of guilt. Many players and reviewers have pointed to the difficulty of slaying the colossi but their concerns centre not on problems with the combat mechanics or the game's control systems, but instead draw attention to the fact that they simply do not want to kill the lumbering giants (see Sherman, 2006). Importantly, the colossi are unwittingly evil, controlled by an unseen hand, and their characters are drawn with maturity and richness that capture their confusion, clumsiness and, on occasions, reluctance to fight. These are not typically aggressive videogame enemies fuelled by an irredeemable amorality that sees them seek out their quarry at all costs. Indeed, some colossi attempt to flee rather than battle and must be engaged in combat by the player who strikes the first blow. Even upon completing the task of dispatching all sixteen of the behemoths, the player does not emerge as the archetypal hero but is awash with uncomfortable feelings of remorse and uncertainty. In its painting of characters with depth, light and shade, *Shadow of the Colossus* is reminiscent of the work of Hayao Miyazaki, whose feature-length anime such as *Princess Mononoke* depict similarly ambiguous characters that are neither wholly good nor evil and are rounded in a manner uncommon in much mainstream animation.

Refusing to yield its secrets to the last, *Shadow of the Colossus* is a remarkably enigmatic game. Though Sony has made copious reference to the team's previous game in the marketing of *Shadow of the Colossus*, the question as to whether this is a sequel, or even prequel, to *Ico* remains tantalisingly unanswered. Hints abound and the culmination of the game sees the appearance of a child with horns like that at the centre of *Ico*'s storyline, while from certain vantage points, *Ico*'s castle seems to be faintly visible on the horizon linking the narratives and spaces of the two titles. Designer Fumito Ueda refuses to be drawn on the exact nature of the connection between the games and their narratives preferring to note that 'There's no specific connection as far as a timeline. But, both games exist in the same world.'[52] Regardless of its relationship to *Ico*, *Shadow of the Colossus* has been fêted by reviewers and critics and has earned numerous awards including Game of the Year at the 2006 Game Developers Choice Awards.[53]

52. <www.wired.com/news/technology/0,70286-0.html?tw=rss.culture>.
53. <www.gamechoiceawards.com/pr/pr_2006_0323.htm>.

Publisher: Sony Computer Entertainment Europe; **Platform**: Sony PlayStation 2.

Shenmue
2000
Sega AM2

By any measure, *Shenmue* is a game of epic scale. Even before play starts, it is an overwhelming experience with a package containing a full four Dreamcast disks (even *Final Fantasy VII*, that poster-child of expansive gaming, took just three CDs to contain it). On beginning the game, however, the scope of *Shenmue*'s extraordinary ambition becomes immediately apparent. On one level, *Shenmue* can be seen as a relatively straightforward role-playing game (RPG) in which the player takes on the part of Ryo avenging the death of his father. Described in this way, not only does the game seem less than revolutionary, but also appears clichéd and tired. Yet even a detailed transcription of the game's backstory captures little of the game's distinctiveness. Indeed, *Shenmue* does not seek to distinguish itself by the length or even complexity of its narrative, or the depth and maturity of its characterisations, though both of these are surely impressive. Rather, in *Shenmue*, designer Yu Suzuki seeks to create a wholly immersive environment – a true virtual world – in which these twisting adventures take place. To illustrate the uniqueness of *Shenmue* and to distinguish his creation from 'mere' RPGs, Suzuki coined the term FREE (Free Reactive Eyes Entertainment) and, while there is a sense that the acronym may have preceded the explanation, it does convey the matchless sense of openness and FREEdom that *Shenmue* offers the player. The intricacy and attention to detail of the modelling of the labyrinthine backstreets, and the wealth of non-playable, incidental characters going about their daily business without directly impacting upon the story, lend *Shenmue*'s Japan a believability and create a real sense of presence in Ryo's lifeworld.

What is most interesting, however, is the game's understatement. Though there are attention-grabbing sequences of great action, including an exuberant and celebratory seventy-man fight towards the end of the game, the majority of the experience is dull and even mundane. And so, a decade and a half before *Animal Crossing*, *Shenmue* showed players that dull and mundane can be utterly beguiling and can create presence and immersion in a virtual world just as effectively as huge explosions and non-stop action. Although *Shenmue* began its life as *Virtua Fighter RPG*,[54] and is suffused with the imagery and influence of this title, it eschews the continuous freneticism of its forebear in favour of a more measured tempo that sees the player actively seeking out diversions to occupy themselves while waiting for an appointment with a character, for example. Similarly, rather than simply reward the player with money for success in battle as in many RPGs, *Shenmue* demands that Ryo get a job to earn his passage. And lest we think that any unnecessary glamour has crept into the game, Ryo does not become a croupier in a casino or racing driver, but rather spends his time shifting boxes in a warehouse as a forklift operator.

Shenmue's most significant contribution to game design is not simply to put its focus as much on the spaces 'between' the set-piece action sequences as on the spectacular fights themselves, but to integrate the two. In order to effect this synthesis, Suzuki's team implemented a system called 'QTE' (Quick Time Events) that sought to blur the boundary between sequences of non-playable exposition and those of play and performance. Games such as *Final Fantasy VII* and *Metal Gear Solid* move the player between positions of play/spectatorship with lavishly pre-rendered movie sequences or 'cut scenes' and their aesthetic difference immediately signals to the player that their input is not required. *Shenmue* provides no such respite. Not only does it make use of the in-game graphics engine for its exposition sequences thereby eradicating any obvious or jarring shift in representational style, but also QTEs frequently interrupt what seem like non-playable sequences and immediately demand player input. In this way, *Shenmue* plays with the structures and modalities of RPGs and refuses to let players' attentions drift.

A sequel was released for Dreamcast and Xbox that continued the storyline, taking Ryo to Hong Kong. Just as with *Shenmue* before, the sequel's ending has prompted considerable speculation of a further instalment.

54. Upon completion of the game's sequel, *Shenmue II*, a video sequence is unlocked that illustrates the unreleased Saturn development of the game. Throughout *Shenmue* and its sequel, *VF* characters appear on posters and in the form of collectible toys available from coin-operated machines in shops.

Publisher: Sega; **Platform**: Sega Dreamcast.

Sid Meier's Civilization[55]
1991
MicroProse

As its title might suggest, *Sid Meier's Civilization* is a game with grand ambitions. Its scale and scope are quite unlike most other videogames, with a canvas that reaches across space and time to cover not only the entire globe, but the course of history over the last 6,000 years. From the earliest days of titles such as *Space Invaders*, videogames have cast their players in roles of great power and responsibility that see them single-handedly accountable for their own destiny and, more often than not, the fate of the entire planet. *Civilization* makes such games look positively modest and the position in which it places its player is sure to give even the humblest of individuals a Messianic complex as they become the unelected leader of an entire civilization for all time. Even the most despotic of rulers could only dream of such omnipotence and would surely envy the absolute power wielded by the player as they manage their economy, engage in diplomacy or wage war, dictate the building of cities and the development of technologies to advance their civilisation.

All of this is played out as a turn-based strategy game that is similar in many regards to board games such as *Risk* save for the fact that it is significantly more complex and requires the management and consideration of many more systems and variables. For a number of commentators, such as Ted Friedman (2002), however, *Civilization* is ultimately about the conquering and mastering of territory and the game is essentially the story of the map as it unfolds over time, gradually becoming visible as it is explored and annexed by the player. Indeed, the game is ultimately not even a simple land rush for Earthly space and victory may be secured by colonising outer space and starting the process of expanding the Empire to Alpha Centauri. In this way, as the player-as-ruler seeks to conquer the world or rid it of all other civilisations, the game promotes a fairly uncomplicated expansionist and imperialistic ideal that might make scholars of postcolonial theory a little uneasy.

Interestingly, while *Civilization* and its increasingly more complex sequels have been enormously popular with players, the games have also found a place in classrooms as tools with which to teach history and the interconnections between economics, politics and geography, for example. However, the games raise a number of concerns also. In addition to the issues of colonisation and materialism, *Civilization* places great emphasis on the role of technology and casts it as a prime agent for social and cultural change. Such technological determinism not only elides the possibility of a more nuanced consideration of the ways in which technology, society and culture are related, but also deprivileges the role of individuals in history, requiring discussion about the incompleteness of the simulation model in *Civilization* and the ways in which it might support or reproduce discourses of progress and western notions of history. As Jenkins and Squire (2003) note in their examination of *Civilization III*, 'There is no such thing as a neutral simulation; they all embody assumptions about the way the world works.'

55. The game is usually known simply as *Civilization* or even just *Civ* among fans.

Publisher: MicroProse; **Platform**: PC, Macintosh, Commodore Amiga.

SimCity
1989
Maxis

SimCity was the first significantly commercially successful videogame that wasn't really a game. While using the map editor he had made for his first title, *Raid on Bungeling Bay*, designer Will Wright found he was getting far more satisfaction out of designing the levels than playing the actual game. Thus, the popular simulation was born.

SimCity offers a simulation system in which the players can set challenges for themselves. It presents an accurate urban planning and development model and purely, simply invites the player to build. The player takes control over zoning land areas (residential, industrial, commercial), maintaining power lines, transport infrastructure – essentially all of the variables that make up the anatomy of a modern city. Despite its functional top-down graphics and the absence of any discernible goal, the game proved to be a sales phenomenon when released for the PC in 1989.

Despite being supplied with no apparent directions for the player, the game did allow the loading of some predetermined scenarios to be played out. This set of prescribed planning nightmares, such as gridlock, flooding and monster attack, provided the player with a refreshing (and often amusing) narrative framework within which to do their remodelling.

Perhaps the greatest legacy of the game, though, has been the passing of the prefix 'Sim' into videogame and, to a large extent, popular parlance. The game spawned a number of further *SimCity* titles, but more worryingly appeared to give licence to almost any noun to be prefixed with the word 'Sim' and turned into a videogame. *SimCopter*, *SimAnt*, *SimFarm*, *SimLife*, *SimIsle*, *SimTower* and perhaps most suspiciously *SimTown* (*SimCity*, but smaller) were all shamelessly released. Again, the mark of true cultural significance, the game found itself parodied in a number of other titles. Most notably, UK developer

Sensible Software released *SimBrick*, in which the user is invited to press a key, whereupon a brick falls upon an ant on screen.

The *Sim* concept reached its natural conclusion when, in 2000, Maxis released *The Sims*, Wright's 'people simulator'. This wildly successful title became the best-selling PC game of all time and was succeeded by *The Sims 2*. Will Wright has since moved on from the franchise to work on a new game, *Spore*, which deals with the creation and population of entire universes. The game, which feels like the (real) final conclusion of the *Sim* project, has been affectionately dubbed 'SimEverything'.

Publisher: Brøderbund; **Platform**: Commodore 64, Commodore Amiga, Atari ST, MS-DOS, Macintosh.

SingStar
2004
Sony Computer Entertainment Europe

SingStar is a product of the confluence of two trends in the videogames industry. First, it is a clear and erudite attempt to broaden the audience for videogames by making them accessible and easy to play. Second, it is fun. In a world of World War II real-time strategy games, stealthy action-adventure experiences and car-driving simulations that allow the player to tweak every aspect of their souped-up car, one could be forgiven for thinking that videogames might be beginning to take themselves a little too seriously. Like the various *EyeToy: Play* games, *SingStar* cannot be accused of being self-obsessed nor does it allow the player to make anything other than a spectacle of themselves. Better still, although there

SingStar: the party game par excellence

is a single-player option, the game is fundamentally a multiplayer experience in which a whole host of friends make fools of themselves in front of one another. 'Pass the mic' mode allows up to eight players to compete against one another in a series of challenges. *SingStar* is a party game par excellence.

It is a simple premise. Take Karaoke and . . . well, actually, *SingStar* is pretty much just Karaoke. A roster of original artists' music, complete with music videos, plays out on screen, with lyrics overlaid, and the players sing along using the two supplied microphones that attach to the PlayStation 2's surprisingly underused USB ports. Importantly, *SingStar*'s microphones not only amplify the players' voices and mix them with the pre-recorded backing tracks but also allow the pitch and rhythm of the performances to be digitised and analysed. As such, the crowd of people gathered around the PlayStation are not the only judges and the game itself evaluates and rates the show, with scores awarded for tuning and timing. To add to the fun, *SingStar* players can make use of the PlayStation 2 EyeToy camera so that they can see their own performances on screen.

SingStar has become a valuable franchise for Sony and a number of themed editions, including Rock and 80s versions, have been released each offering a new selection of songs to croon along with. Critical and commercial success means that *SingStar* is an important series and intellectual property in its own right but, perhaps even more significantly, the game sits alongside *EyeToy: Play* and *Buzz* as part of Sony's push to rid videogaming of its geeky associations and turn it into a viable, fun and even chic form of entertainment for twenty-somethings. The array of 'lifestyle' images available at Sony Computer Entertainment Europe's online press office are an eloquent, if rather mannered, expression of this intention and show a group of beautiful people enjoying *SingStar* in their stylish, modern flat.[56] Moreover, *SingStar* is one of the few videogames to have been explicitly marketed at women and girls, with advertisements appearing in *heat* magazine, for example. Ultimately, while the licensing of music and video from top artists is doubtless a contributing factor, *SingStar* succeeds because of the simplicity of its execution. It is immediate and understandable and has a clean hardware and software interface that does not get in the way of the fun and sociality that it fosters. As with so many party (video)games, *SingStar* is a catalyst for fun. It creates a playful environment in which there are pleasures to be had in playing, judging or watching.

56. <www.scee.presscentre.com/imagelibrary/default.asp?SubjectID=1477>.

Publisher: Sony Computer Entertainment; **Platform**: Sony PlayStation 2.

Sissyfight
2000
Eric Zimmerman

One of the first online browser-based games to achieve any kind of real 'cult' status, *Sissyfight* is a peculiar mix of design styles, both visual and ludic. Built on the Macromedia Shockwave platform, the game ran embedded in web browsers and was one of the first examples of networked shockwave play. Arguably, it was a very early MMOG (Massively Multiplayer Online Game). Designed by 'proper' game studies academic Eric Zimmerman, the rules are simple but demand a good deal of strategic planning (or strategic alliances) in order to secure a win. The game takes place in the world of the schoolgirl playground, which is drawn in a pastel-hued version of the popular 8-bit pixel-art style.

The rules of *Sissyfight* are simple, the premise is imbued with the casual cruelty of childhood. Up to six girls compete against each other online in an attempt to destroy the self-esteem of each other. In turn-based play, each girl must choose the move they will make and against which other player. The girls are able to scratch, tease and tattle on each other with upsetting effect. There tends to always be more than one winner.

Sissyfight is a curious hybrid of game and chat room. With players able to openly chat to each other within the game, a vicious internal dialogue often rapidly breaks out. This is usually an extraordinarily cruel stream of deeply creative insults as players free-associate their profanities into lyrical barbs of filth. This truly is the playground manifest.

At its height, *Sissyfight* was a hugely popular destination and was one of the first truly visible examples of casual gameplay. Central to its success, though, is the deep emotional reaction it appears to provoke in players. It is truly a far crueller place than a *Quake* deathmatch, as intricate, delicate but very short-lived political structures are built and forgotten within the space of a game. It's incredibly emotionally charged. Perhaps not surprisingly then, the game came in for harsh criticism from parents' groups who felt that the game was encouraging that sort of behaviour in their young. Zimmerman was equivocal in his defence,

> The human psyche does not work on a monkey-see, monkey-do basis, *Sissyfight* is radically metaphorical, voluntarily entered into and satisfyingly transgressive. The idea that play should be 'good for you' and turn you into a better citizen of the state is something that I want to question.[57]

57. <archive.salon.com/tech/feature/2000/04/27/sissyfight/index.html>.

Publisher: Word; **Platform**: Shockwave.

Snake
1997
Taneli Armanto

There will be few who would doubt that the simplest ideas are often the best and, in the world of videogames, ideas don't come much simpler than *Snake*. Graphically, the game is extraordinarily simple. Economical to the point of abstract beauty, the screen is occupied by little more than the eponymous snake that grows ever longer as time progresses – though quite how or why this expansion takes place is never explained. The narrative, if we can call it such, does not extend to explication or backstory. Rather, all we know is that, in search of an on screen block of indeterminate character that is possibly food, the snake roams relentlessly through the bounded play space contained by the physical border of the display. The snake's only purpose in life appears to be to keep moving so as to find more food and grow yet longer. And like so much in life, it is precisely that which the snake wants that is its downfall as it has to at all costs avoid bumping into itself as this spells inevitable and instant death. If a snake could have an Achilles heel, then its perpetual motion would be it. As an animal lover, your task as player is to help the snake extend its life by guiding it around the screen, steering by the head, and most importantly charting a path that ensures that it avoids its ever-growing tail. Unfortunately, the death of the snake is inevitable. Like many 1970s and 1980s game designs, the player, and in this case the snake, cannot win. Success in the game only prolongs the inevitable demise. This structure betrays the game's heritage as, although it leaped to prominence in the 1990s, *Snake* has existed in some guise or other for three decades doing the rounds of home computers and being ported to almost every format imaginable under a range of serpent-themed names as though to feign originality or mask plagiarism.

While remarkably efficient and delightfully simple, *Snake*'s game design is not the best idea here. In fact, as with so many apparently great and simple ideas, its exquisitely refined gameplay, graphics and sound are the consequence of technical limitation. Necessity is the mother of invention, after all. 1970s computing technology may have seemed like science fiction at the time, offering a glimpse into a hitherto unimagined world but we are well advised to remember that the ability to render anything with any degree of visual flair was a considerable challenge. Couple this with the problem of placing these graphical representations under the control of the player, and any genuine and convincing interactivity success was a significant achievement. This is not to say that the fun that emerges from such limited technology is not testimony to the considerable imagination of game designers, but rather that it serves as a reminder that when we look at games such as *Snake* through eyes that have become accustomed to and blasé about photo-realism, we perhaps forget that excellence in game design really was all there was to work with. Without a compelling game, what was there? The phrase 'eye candy' would not trouble the prose of videogame reviewers for some years to come. So, if efficient game design and unbridled fun are not the stroke of genius here, then what is?

The really great idea that beats at the heart of *Snake* is the decision to charm it away from home computers and TV displays and place it on the screen of a mobile phone. Nokia have kept this snake alive far longer than any player has ever managed. They did not invent the game, but as Nintendo did with *Tetris*, they have created its most perfect implementation. By embedding the game into the Nokia 6110 and subsequent handsets, *Snake* ensured that the mobile phone would become the most ubiquitous handheld gaming platform. All the PlayStation Portables and Nintendo DS consoles do not come close to the number of Nokia handsets all sitting in quiet anticipation of their menus being set to 'Game'.

What makes *Snake* so perfect a companion to the mobile phone is that, like *Pong* and so many of its 1970s brethren, it makes little demand on the host hardware. While mobile phones may boggle us with their technical sophistication and offer apparent glimpses into a future of technological superiority, just as early home computers did in decades past, they are, in truth, limited gaming platforms. Audiovisually they are the inferior of dedicated handheld gaming devices such as GameBoy but *Snake* is beautifully scalable and does not require colour or elaborate animation. But for gamers, it is in their hardware interfaces that mobile phones are weakest. There are few imagined futures in which keys numbered nought to nine replace the joypad. What makes *Snake* so utterly perfect a mobile phone game is that it demands so simple a hardware interface. Up, down, left, right. That is all. Fortunate perhaps, as this is almost all the phone has to offer, but that is all that is required. And so nothing is missing, nothing is cut down, nothing offered in 'lite' form. This is *Snake* as originally intended.

Further demonstrating the fusion of game and platform, this most durable of games, which so ably matches hardware to design, is just perfect for opportunistic play. It suits short play sessions, snatched when the opportunity arises. It is unlikely to be a game that maintains attention for many hours or that one would deliberately set aside time to play in the evening, for example. However, those moments waiting for a bus, travelling on a train, or waiting in the dentist's waiting room can all pass just a little faster in the company of your trusty mobile phone and a stretchy serpent. Saving snakes is a great way to kill time.

Publisher: Nokia; **Platform**: Nokia 6110.

Sonic the Hedgehog
1991
Sonic Team

Throughout the 1980s and early 1990s, Nintendo were the dominant force in home console videogaming. The release of the Nintendo Entertainment System had not only rejuvenated the company, making their name synonymous with gaming, but had also kickstarted the previously moribund videogames industry as a whole.[58] Key to Nintendo's success had been the *Super Mario* series and so well loved were the games that the titular character had moved from in-game protagonist to become a corporate mascot who spoke of the fun and family-orientation of Nintendo's products. *Sonic the Hedgehog* was a self-conscious attempt on Sega's part to create a competing mascot with which they could attempt to loosen the stranglehold that Nintendo had over the home videogames market. Looking rather more like Felix the cat

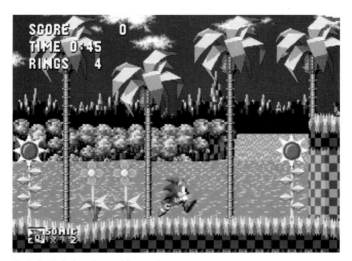

Sonic the Hedgehog: the need for speed

than a hedgehog,[59] Sonic was designed to be inclusive and appeal to as wide a cross-section of the potential gaming audience as possible.[60] What is most important, however, is the way in which Sonic came to embody the corporate ideals and technologies of his parent company.

Where Super Mario's bright, bold, primary-coloured worlds perfectly communicated the child-friendliness of Nintendo and his games privileged exploration and adventuring, Sonic was brash and edgy. Indeed, in advertising and marketing materials, he was referred to as a 'hedgehog with attitude'. Most importantly, though, Sonic is fast – supersonic, in fact. Super Mario is many things, but he is never in a hurry. Sonic, by contrast, is a blur of blue spines and power sneakers. Speed not only differentiated the gameplay of these two standard-bearing games, but also came to characterise the qualities and capabilities of Sega's Megadrive console. Wearing its technical credentials proudly on its sleeve with '16-Bit' emblazoned in gold lettering on the top of the otherwise black console, the MegaDrive belonged to the 'next generation' of processing, graphics and audio power and Sega's marketing took great pains to point out the technological superiority of their device in comparison with Nintendo's aging 8-bit NES.

More persuasive than any amount of technical specifications and arguing about bits, bytes and processor cycles per second, however, was the sheer pace at which *Sonic the Hedgehog* played. Ostensibly a similar experience to *Super Mario Bros*, in being a platform game that presented the player with a virtual obstacle course and gave them the task of battling from the beginning to the end of a raft of increasingly complicated levels, *Sonic the Hedgehog*'s environments were richly detailed. Drawing on a colour palette that accentuates the deep blues of the sky and the lush greens of the verdant Emerald zone, the gameworld had extraordinary depth as scenery stretched out towards the horizon, each layer scrolling with a smooth parallax effect that lent the world a solidity and three-dimensionality. Such was the speed of the game that on many occasions the action was literally out of control with the hedgehog spinning and rolling around loop-the-loops and flying off ramps high into the sky as the player tried desperately to keep pace. Embracing this yet further, one level is set in a gigantic pinball machine and bumpers, flippers and springs send Sonic bouncing about in a curled-up blue ball. The message is clear, and old-fashioned pinball and platform games get a supercharged boost courtesy of Sega's new high-tech, next-generation console. Such is Sonic's impatience and need for speed that if he is left unattended for more than a few seconds, he turns to face the player and taps on the inside of the screen, before eventually falling asleep.[61]

Sonic the Hedgehog enjoyed a number of MegaDrive sequels that built upon the basic gameplay and added new characters and levels to explore. Today, Sonic remains a valuable property for Sega and he features in many series spanning a range of genres.

58. See Sheff (1993) for more on the history of Nintendo and their rise to ascendancy.
59. C. David and B. Shoemaker (n.d.).
60. See Eisenberg (1998).
61. Mario would go on to perform a very similar behaviour in Super Mario 64 and makes himself comfortable on the ground, snoozing and even talking in his sleep if left by the player.

Publisher: Sega; **Platform**: Sega MegaDrive.

Space Invaders
1978
Taito

It was not the graphics, not even the narrative that placed you as the Earth's sole hope against an alien attack, but the electronic heartbeat that created the sense of foreboding. The almost subsonic beating spoke of the living, breathing, organic aliens. More pertinently, the pulsing perfectly matched the pace of the attack, raising the tension and anxiety in time with the escalating onslaught of the alien Other.

Of course, the job of winning the hearts and minds of the playing public in these early days of videogames was made rather easier for the aliens given that outer space and science fiction had become rather fashionable in the late 1970s. The release of *Star Wars* had seen to that and the mania that surrounded Lucas's first trilogy doubtless fanned the flames of *Space Invaders* hysteria. Interestingly, though, recalling the visual development of the game in 2005, Toshihiro Nishikado, the game's designer, cites a rather more classic source of inspiration. After initial attempts to draw the enemy as aeroplanes had been scuppered by limited graphics technology, and opposed to allowing players to engage in the immorality of shooting other humans, H. G. Wells's vivid descriptions of octopus-like invaders took hold.[62] It is curious to note then that its hostile, alien-infested outer-space setting that is the very defining feature of the game was not a conscious design decision taken at the outset of development but rather a product of technical limitation and compromise.

Viewed with today's eyes, the lure of *Space Invaders* is perhaps a little hard to discern and the multicoloured strips placed over the black and white screen to fake the effect of technicolour lend the game a retro chic but may also locate it firmly in another age. Like many games of its era, there is no variation in the gameplay. What the player sees on first sight is all they can ever expect with no detours, no multiple levels, no variable attack patterns. The game puts the player in charge of a laser cannon that can travel only left and right along the bottom of the screen

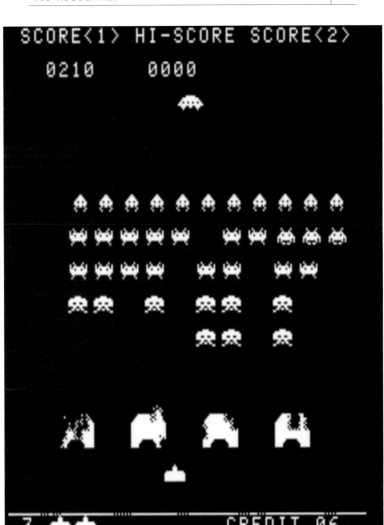

Space Invaders: the alien Other

and pits them against wave upon wave of the eponymous aggressors, neatly arranged in rows and columns. The precision of their formations served only to further code them as inhuman or even drones controlled by a yet more potent but unseen force. Certainly, something was afoot and millions of people all over the world, perhaps equally drone-like, rushed to pump coins into the machine that soon became the most popular and successful videogame to date. Such was the passion for the game that it was held responsible for a shortage of yen in Japan as so much of the currency sat in the coin boxes of *Space Invaders* machines in arcades.

Space Invaders' legacy is considerable. Not only did it normalise the mechanic of infinite ammunition and a game structure that could only end in the player's defeat and the invasion of the Earth, it raised the visibility and popularity of videogames as a cultural form across the globe and was at least partly responsible for bringing them to the mass market. However, less positively, *Space Invaders* was also surrounded by controversy and the moral panics that still accompany gaming abounded even in these early days with talk of addiction and theft to fuel the 'habit'. In the UK, 1981 saw Labour MP George Foulkes table the 'Control of Space Invaders (and other Electronic Games) Bill', which traded on the putative link between videogames and delinquency, and was only narrowly defeated (Haddon, 1988: 60).

62. See Edge-Online. Available at <www.edge-online.co.uk/archives/2005/10/ taito_men_talk.php>.

Publisher: Midway; **Platform**: Coin-Op.

Spheres of Chaos
2003
Iain McLeod

Spheres of Chaos is, at heart, a simple and elegant *Asteroids* clone. The function of the game is simple enough and, while bringing some innovations to the *Asteroids* game by way of cycling power-ups, *SoC* is most notable for the frequent occasions when the function is completely hidden by the form. Clearly influenced by the work of Jeff Minter, this shareware title takes Minter's psychedelic visual style and amplifies it beyond the point where it is augmenting any gameplay. *SoC* allows the shimmering particle effects to completely obfuscate the actual game and change the player's experience from one of gaming, into one of synaesthetic pleasure.

The configuration options of the game offer a startling variety of choices, in particular in the visual presentation. Such is the breadth of

Spheres of Chaos: the pleasures of synaesthesia

different rendering options that can be selected, *SoC* can transform itself into a wholly different game by choosing a differing setting. In some of its more extreme/sublime configurations, the game washes away the rigid form of the shooter under waves of abstract colour; *SoC* invites the player to paint – rather than destroy – with their bullets. In many respects, a good game of *SoC* apes the structure of a number of films that have attempted to relate the narcotic experience, beginning within formal, rational worlds and then proceeding to gradually collapse into hallucination. What's so interesting about *SoC* is exactly that – it's a gradual collapse – the game cross-fades into psychedelia before your eyes.

The sonic design of the game also deserves singling out for attention. Never, ever silent, *SoC* mostly eschews traditional sonic effects for resonant, pitched bells. Aliens don't just explode, they ring at random pitches. While everything visual is approaching mayhem around the player, these oddly hypnotic sounds have the strange effect of decelerating the actual gametime.

SoC fills you with joy at the realisation you're playing something as it was intended. The sheer *abandon* of those effects and the obvious absence of any external, more commercially minded, interference to tone them down is joyous to behold. This is how it was meant to be, and it's intoxicating to be swept along in the audacity of that vision. Of course, this complete abandon to visual excess could probably only occur within the shareware arena and it's here that the game has found its home. *SoC* represents all that is great about independent, 'homebrew' game design. Its flaws, and there are many quite fundamental ones, are a part of its appeal. Focus-testing might have rendered the text in the high-score table legible beneath the wash of particle effects, but it would have subtracted from its character. It stands as a reminder of a period of games development where the authorial signature was more often visible.

Publisher: N/A; **Platform**: Windows, Linux, PS2 Linux, RISC OS.

Spider-Man 2
2004
Treyarch

On a clear day, from the top of the Empire State Building you can see Manhattan Island stretch away to the north, almost making out the south end of Central Park. This isn't any city, New York is pivotal to this particularly pop-culture mythology. A *Spider-Man* story can't play out against an anonymous metropolis or symbolic Gotham, it's a specific local context for the super-hero most likely to suffer from banal interventions in his adventures.

This 'official movie merchandise' to the 2004 film of the same name is decisively focused on the importance of the city. The convention of the movie-licence game to date has usually been to offer a gameplay experience that closely mirrors the narrative of the source film, borrowing source art and buying in actors' voice talents. Refreshingly (and partly out of necessity – the developers weren't privy to the film until late in the development process) for a major movie licence, Treyarch opted not to attempt to recreate a narrative, but to enable the player to inhabit the character and his extraordinary abilities in his local environment. *Spider-Man 2* the videogame isn't about *Spider-Man 2* the movie, it's about playing at *Spider-Man* in a contemporary Manhattan. Control and context are all.

In recreating a contemporary New York, Treyarch have wisely opted for an economy of realisation in their design. The game (and hardware platforms, at the time of release) isn't able, nor is it attempting to, create a photo-realistic architecturally accurate model of the city. Unlike the declared ambition of Sony Computer Entertainment Europe's *The Getaway* and its labours to create a wholly accurate model of an area of London, *SM2* is more measured, albeit with a rather larger canvas, electing to provide only the most recognisable way-points for the player to orientate themselves by. Buildings of particular resonance are detailed – the Flatiron building, Central Park, the Empire State are all rendered for exploration. In distilling New York City into its most iconic architectural features, the game succeeds in sustaining a real feeling of presence in the 'actual' city. Meeting the sensitivities of recent history directly, the game includes memorial beacons at Ground Zero that illuminate as the sun sets. The game makes no attempt to simulate a 'living' city, with the complex causalities we might expect from a Will Wright opus – *SM2* does not make any attempt to behave like a complex city, in doing so it succeeds in feeling like one.

But having the expanse of the city to play with is nothing without the means to traverse it. *SM2* invested heavily in a redesigning of the central swinging mechanic from the previous title. Like the best control schemes, it is simple in its essence, but rewards practice by allowing the player to perform beautifully animated feats of aerial acrobatics. The variety and precision of control that a player can develop generates a euphoric state of flow that has been rarely matched. Much of the critical reception commented on the speed, the 'rush' of flying through and around the city. Throwing oneself from the height of a skyscraper in order to 'sling' a webline moments before hitting the sidewalk is one of the undeclared user-created mini-games. The game invites and helps the player to appear graceful, and regularly rewards your abilities with even more power-ups – locking one into a loop of gratification.

The game stalls most when compared against its most obvious influence, the free-roaming city and mission structure of *Grand Theft Auto*. Some alarmingly difficult tasks are set the player mid-way through the game, which result in some players experiencing 'shelf-level' events, in which the task is so hard that the player is removed from the action. This in turn leads to the game being removed from the console and placed on the shelf, from where it may never return.

Publisher: Activision; **Platform**: Microsoft Xbox, Nintendo GameCube, Sony PlayStation 2.

Street Fighter II
1991
Capcom

Although it belongs to a wholly different genre, Capcom's *Street Fighter II* (*SFII*) bears much in common with games such as *Asteroids* and *Space Invaders*. All are complex games with a depth that reveals itself on successive play and that demands tactics and strategy, but all are unremittingly single-minded in their focus. Where *Asteroids* and *Space Invaders* are concerned solely with shooting, *SFII* is about bare-knuckle fighting. Nothing more, nothing less. It is a remarkably simple formula. Two players are pitted against one another and the last standing is declared the winner. There are no hordes of oncoming attackers, no outlandish weapons (save for fireballs) and, as a result, combat is almost myopically focused on the single opponent that stands in the way and takes place for the most part at close quarters. And while there can be little doubt that *SFII* is a vicious and unrelenting experience, it is no mindless bout of ultraviolence. This brutal ballet of punches and kicks is executed with a passion and purity that demands both discipline and dedication and rewards grace and thoughtfulness rather than maniacal thuggery or random button-bashing.

As its name suggests, *SFII* was not Capcom's first foray into the fighting genre. The original *Street Fighter* launched in 1987, riding the wave of popularity created by Data East's *Karate Champ* and Konami's *Yie Ar Kung-Fu*. Capcom's offering made little impression on players as it was a poorly balanced game in which the playable characters' signature moves were fiendishly difficult to execute yet so deadly that if they could be performed, they would bring the game to an almost immediate end. Nonetheless, lurking under this unpromising surface were some of the qualities and principles that would make the sequel so compelling and revolutionary. A roster of eight playable characters from which the player could choose was introduced as six new fighters joined Ken and Ryu, the protagonists from the first game. A further four non-playable characters or 'Bosses' were available for those tackling the single-player mode.

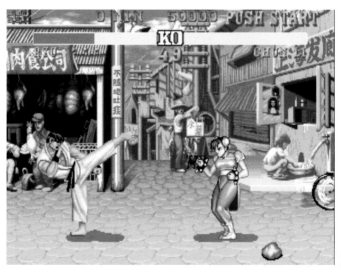

Street Fighter II: a brutal ballet of punches, kicks and fireballs

Crucially, each character fought with their own style and, importantly, possessed a unique set of moves and capabilities. Key to the success of the sequel was the level matching of the various characters; some were agile and quick with comparatively weak attacks that encouraged and facilitated an offensive style, while others were cumbersome and lumbering but with devastatingly effective moves that demanded a more cautiously defensive strategy. The strongest attacks demanded considerable knowledge of the game's control systems as they were not widely publicised or included in the game's instructions. Moreover, chaining moves together to create an unblockable composite of attacks, known as a 'combo', required great dexterity and extraordinary timing. This complexity and depth have ensured that *Street Fighter II* has maintained a devout following keen to demonstrate their skills and knowledge of the game.[63]

Just as *SFII* was not Capcom's first fighting game, it was certainly not their last and the game is notable for the sheer number of sequels, spin-offs and derivatives that it has spawned. Such is the technical nature of the game that apparently minor variations often have a profound impact on play. Accordingly, the timing of combos, for example, or tweaks to the matching of characters to level the playing field, are as potentially significant as the introduction of new characters or changes to background graphics. Sequels and spin-offs number in the tens, each with increasingly complicated and esoteric suffixes that contribute to the game's 'hardcore' status: *Championship Edition*; *Special Championship Edition*; and *Hyper Fighting*. To confuse matters further, the games are often retitled in different territories: *Super Street Fighter II Turbo: Grand Master Challenge* is known as *Super Street Fighter II X* in Japan and is, itself, a slightly reworked version of *Super Street Fighter II: The New Challengers*. More recently, Capcom has turned its attention to retrospective collections of various *SFII* games and a VS series that pits *SFII* characters against those from other company's fighting games (such as SNK) or even characters from Marvel comics.

Almost every console and handheld has been treated to a port of at least one version of *SFII* and its successors and during Sega and Nintendo's console battle in the 1990s, the game was a key licence. Indeed in the UK, the SNES version became notorious not only for its quality but also for its £70 price tag that made it roughly twice as expensive as most other games and almost as costly as the console on which it ran.

63. See <www.shoryuken.com/wiki/index.php/Strategy_Guide> for examples of strategy guides and a notation system for moves.

Publisher: Capcom; **Platform**: Coin-Op.

Super Mario 64
1996 (Japan, US); 1997 (Europe)
Nintendo EAD

The term 'genre-defining' is overused in videogaming parlance, with almost every game claiming to push back the boundaries of the form in some way. In the case of *Super Mario 64*, however, the phrase is not only appropriate but may even underestimate the importance and impact of the title. Just prior to its launch in 1996, Hiroshi Yamauchi was in little doubt of the game's greatness. 'I don't mean to brag, but when this game is finished I believe it will be our best ever.'[64] Yet even he couldn't predict the accolades and praise that would be heaped upon the title or that it would remain consistently in the upper echelons of 'best game of all time' polls.[65]

SM64's influence and innovation is difficult to isolate. Visually, it added a new dimension to platform games, taking them from 2D linear obstacle courses, to explorations of and journeys through 3D space. From a game design perspective, its use of a central hub structure with radiating levels and courses has been much mimicked, while it's the way it encourages players to revisit and explore spaces, levels and worlds, revealing something different each time, that is matchless. Its tantalising glimpses of the goal and task of each stage delivered by a flythrough of the level ensures the player is never left floundering or uncertain as to their goal, yet the avoidance of overt didacticism or spoon-feeding leaves them feeling autonomous and in control. And 'control' is the keyword in *SM64*.

More than any of these aesthetic, design and structural qualities, it is the synthesis of controller, player and character that makes *SM64* so significant – and durable. To play *SM64* is to experience a connection with the game and an unrivalled feeling of a character – of a world – under your control. Indeed, the game's producer, Shigeru Miyamoto, notes that designing and perfecting the control of Mario was the first and most important task undertaken by the development team, with the remainder of the game being built around this mechanic. This was partly an issue of software design – of translating the control inputs of players into on screen actions – but also a hardware problem. In short, *SM64* could not exist without the N64 controller alongside which it was designed. And yet, the N64 controller is not an inspiring piece of equipment. All design is about compromises, yet there is a palpable tension manifest in the N64 pad design and it clearly sits at the cusp of 2D/3D gaming offering an uncomfortable mix of old and new inputs. Even the different ways in which the pad has to be held – particularly the asymmetric grasp required to play *SM64* and the new breed of 3D games and the need for a fallback position to accommodate 'old school' play styles – speak of a lack of certainty about this new direction. These fears proved unfounded, however, and in affording a precision not previously experienced by gamers, the N64's control pad ensured that 'analog sticks' would become de rigueur for videogames hardware designers.

Super Mario 64: 'I don't mean to brag, but when this game is finished I believe it will be our best ever'. Mr Yamauchi may have been right

While controllers and level design structures may be replicated by other developers, *SM64* is a characteristically 'Nintendo' game. Its bold, bright primary colours evoke childhood and create an accessible, playful world. Moreover, the game takes advantage of Nintendo's extensive gaming heritage and draws heavily on characters and environments from the *Super Mario* universe to create a wholly consistent world. This self-referentiality serves to promote a sense of continuity between this game and its antecedents, simultaneously grounding a revolutionary title within the familiar and promoting Nintendo's prowess in game development. For example, far from trying to hide the in-game camera for fear that it might undermine the integrity of the player's experience, *Super Mario 64* makes explicit play of it, visibly handing the duties of camerawork to the Lakitu Brothers who occasionally interject to offer assistance and whose reflections can be seen in the many mirrors hanging on the castle's walls.

More recently, *SM64* was released as a launch title for the Nintendo DS handheld console and, while its charm and humour remained intact even adding some nods to the vibrant fan culture of rumour and innuendo that have surrounded the game, including the fabled playable character and fellow Mario Brother, Luigi, it did not showcase the innovative hardware as well as titles such as *WarioWare Touched!* or *Yoshi Touch & Go*. Details of the forthcoming *Mario 128* sequel for Nintendo's 'Revolution' console are characteristically vague prior to release.

64. <www.miyamotoshrine.com/kong/features/mario64/index.shtml>.
65. *Super Mario 64* was the first of what remains only five games to receive a perfect 10/10 score from the UK's well-respected *EDGE* magazine (issue 35), while IGN ranked it fifth in their Top 100 Games (<top100.ign.com/2005/001-010.html>) and GameSpot naming it one of the fifteen most influential games of all time (<uk.gamespot.com/gamespot/features/video/15influential/index.html>).

Publisher: Nintendo; **Platform**: Nintendo 64.

Super Mario Bros.
1985 (Japan, US); 1987 (Europe)
Nintendo

It is unusual to find a media text that is both critically acclaimed and popular. *Super Mario Bros.*, however, is the perfect example. Near-universally fêted by reviewers and appearing at the top of numerous lists of the best ever games,[66] it is also recognised as the best-selling game ever with over 40 million copies sold.[67]

Released in 1985, the game was a launch title for the Nintendo Famicom (renamed Nintendo Entertainment System, and known more

Super Mario Bros.: the best-selling game ever

simply as the NES, outside Japan) and introduced the world to Mario, a character who would, according to David Sheff (1993: 9), become more widely recognised by American children than Mickey Mouse or the President. Although the character had appeared in a previous Nintendo game, *Donkey Kong*, he had been known only as 'Jumpman' until this point. He would also change careers for *Super Mario Bros.*, leaving behind carpentry and becoming the now-familiar plumber. Mario also has a part-time job as the corporate mascot of Nintendo and his beaming visage adorns not only a lucrative series of games including sequels to *Super Mario Bros.*, but also *Super Mario Kart*, and even spin-offs such as *Yoshi Touch & Go*, but also most of the company's corporate communications and PR materials.

Super Mario Bros.' importance does not derive from being the first of its genre. Though it is certainly among the first platform games, it was preceded by at least a year by titles such as Namco's *Pac-Land* that took the familiar yellow, pizza-shaped, eating machine out of his 2D maze and placed him into a scrolling landscape of obstacles and traps. It seems odd to suggest that a genre so young could have been redefined, but such is *Super Mario Bros.*' impact, that this actually undersells its contribution to game design. The game established so many of the principles that still underpin design today that it is highly likely that without it, modern videogames would be very different. If we examine just its use of 'power-ups', we find both innovation and lasting influence. The *Alice in Wonderland*-inspired mushrooms that allow Mario to grow twice his normal size and become 'Super Mario' not only affect gameplay by altering the player's abilities, but also ensure that a single hit from an enemy will not end a game outright but instead will give the player a second chance as Super Mario becomes plain, old, non-super normal-sized Mario. Expanding the possibilities with stars that provide temporary invincibility, flowers that grant the ability to shoot fireballs at enemies, and thereby modifying the set of capabilities the player has in the world, is just one of this game's contributions to the form as a whole.

Super Mario Bros. catapulted its designer, Shigeru Miyamoto, to superstar status and he became one of a number of game development auteurs whose names are widely known among the gaming cognoscenti. Miyamoto would go on to create sequels to *Super Mario Bros.* for all of Nintendo's consoles and handheld devices, as well as a number of other equally well-known series, such as *The Legend of Zelda*.

Although originally released over twenty years ago, *Super Mario Bros.* retains much currency in contemporary game cultures. Not only has the game been re-released as part of the Classic NES Series for GameBoy Advance in 2004, it is also given continued life through the practice of 'speedrunning' in which players attempt to complete the game in the quickest possible time. The fastest speedruns stand at marginally over five minutes for the entire game, which partly reflects the extraordinary skill of the expert super-players, and also another of Miyamoto's influential design decisions. Hidden away in *Super Mario Bros.* are a number of Warp Zones that allow the player to skip ahead to later levels and miss out huge swathes of the game in between. The Warp Zones are both ingenious and well hidden, and push at the boundaries of the gameworld itself and its relationship to the screen. For example, accessing one Warp Zone involves jumping 'out of' the play world and running along the top of the screen, past the end of the level and even past the score before dropping into a secret room of pipes that lead directly to different stages. Even in these early days of videogame development, there is a confidence displayed here and a postmodern playfulness that suggest a maturity beyond the form's years. It is for these reasons, as well as the fact that the game is extremely challenging, not to mention enormous fun, that it will doubtless stay at the top of 'Best Games' lists to come.

66. Online games review network *IGN* placed *Super Mario Bros.* in first place in its 'Top 100 Games of All Time' in both 2003 and 2005 (see <top100.ign.com/2003/1-10.html> and <top100.ign.com/2005/001-010.html>). *Electronic Gaming Monthly* (*EGM*) placed it atop their 'The 200 Greatest Video Games of Their Time' list (see <www.1up.com/do/feature?cId=3147448>).

67. According to the *Guinness Book of Records*, *Super Mario Bros.* has sold 40.23 million copies (<www.guinnessworldrecords.com/content_pages/record.asp?recordid =52404>). Through continued re-releases of the game (for GameBoy, for example), this number is set to continue growing.

Publisher: Nintendo; **Platform**: Nintendo Entertainment System.

Super Mario Kart
1992 (Japan, US); 1993 (Europe)
Nintendo

Super Mario Kart is a racing game with a difference. In fact, it has a
number of differences. First, as its name makes no attempt to hide, it is a
go-kart racing game. Contemporary players may struggle to recognise
the innovation here what with *Crash Bandicoot*, *Spyro the Dragon* and
even *Bomberman* all muscling in on the karting action. But, remember,
these pretenders to the crown are only here because of the enormous
influence of Mario and pals. It is worth noting also that the go-kart is not
an inconsequential choice of vehicle. Most obviously, being low to the
ground and a naturally slippery customer in real life, go-kart handling

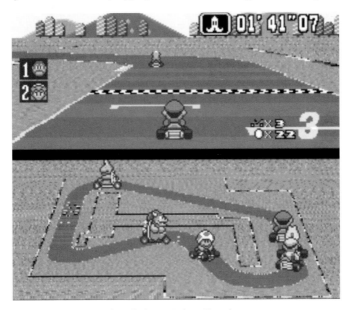

Super Mario Kart: It's not about the karts. It's about Nintendo

immediately lends *SMK* an advantage over rival racing games as powerslides are not simply the mark of the ace driver with hundreds of race laps under their belt, but rather are the standard means of making one's way round a corner. The way the karts handle is so intuitive, so exhilarating, so much fun, which is, of course, the watchword of Nintendo. And this is the real genius of the karts. Without car chassis and hardtop roofs to obscure them, we can see the bevy of Nintendo characters in all their glory. This game is not about the karts; this game is about Nintendo. At every turn, *SMK* is drenched in the imagery and iconography of Nintendo, and this serves not only to create a consistent and coherent world, but reminds you of the fact that few, if any, other developers would be capable of creating such a rich, deep world. *SMK* is one of the most effective corporate marketing tools, not merely because it is a superb game in itself, but because it draws upon and foregrounds the vast back-catalogue of superb games, characters and properties that comprise Nintendo's heritage. The line-up of racers includes the eponymous Mario as well as Donkey Kong, Toad, Princess Peach, Bowser and Koopa, among others, but there is much more. Each character's weaponry is drawn from the *Super Mario* universe and includes Mario's mushrooms and coins, Donkey Kong's bananas and Koopa's shells, while green pipes spring up from the track as obstacles reminding us of the moustachioed plumber's day job. Even before the race starts, we are deep in Nintendo country as Lakitu appears and, where once he was hell-bent on hurling spiked balls at us to stop our progress through *Super Mario Bros.*, here he is still atop his cloud, waving the chequered flag and, because this is Nintendo, everything, including the clouds, wears a beaming smile. This is a game that does not take itself seriously in a way that *Gran Turismo* does. Instead, it is supremely assured and self-confident yet without a trace of arrogance.

It is worth remembering also that *SMK* was something of a technical tour de force also and its use of the SNES console's Mode7 to simulate 3D remains impressive and was jaw-dropping upon release. Moreover, *SMK* drew heavily on Nintendo's experience not only in the use of characters and settings, but also in game design and made great use of devices such as shortcuts that come direct from the lexicon of the platform game. This is hardly surprising given Nintendo's dominance of this genre. If *Super Mario* had revolutionised the platformer, then why not invigorate the racer as well?

SMK has proved an extremely durable and important franchise for Nintendo and, since the original game was released for the SNES in 1992, every one of the company's successful console and heldheld devices has been treated to a version of the game. Most recently, the Nintendo DS has taken *Mario Kart* online, allowing up to four players from across the globe to compete head-to-head. Indeed, such is the title's cachet that Nintendo chose *Mario Kart DS* for their first foray into DS online connectivity. Perhaps because of the matchless handling of the karts, the effortless ease of set-up, or just the pure, unbridled, unmatched fun of *SMK* even thirteen years after we first started powersliding, it has been quite a success with over one million unique players registered within the first four months.[68]

68. Source: Nintendo Wifi Connection News, <www.nintendowifi.com/global/searchArticles.do?article_id=60> (accessed March 2006).

Publisher: Nintendo; **Platform**: Super Nintendo Entertainment System.

Super Monkey Ball
2001
Amusement Vision

If there's one thing almost all videogame critics agree upon, it's that monkeys are brilliant. More often than not, they are also funny. Game developers have also long shown a fascination with simian characters, from the seminal *Donkey Kong* to *The Secret of Monkey Island* to a variety of monkey cameo roles in the acclaimed *Time Splitters* series of games by Free Radical Design. Perhaps the best use of monkey, however, has been in the joyous series of titles from Sega, *Super Monkey Ball*. Such is their innocence, charm and witty invention that they hinted at what 'party games' might be, before Sony had attempted to own the phrase.

Super Monkey Ball is the ludicrous descendant of *Marble Madness*. It's a physics-based game that (in the core mode) challenges you with moving a monkey (in a ball) along a demanding track to reach a prescribed goal (without falling off the edge). In a trait common to many puzzle games, however, *SMB* doesn't enable the player with any control over their avatar in the game. Rather, the player is able to tilt the surface of the world through degrees using the analogue control stick. The monkeys roll where the laws of physics take them, the player controls the terrain.

Super Monkey Ball is rather more than just a *Marble Madness* clone, however. Where it truly excels is in its command of absurd humour, exemplified through the series of mini-games contained within. It is here that the party truly begins. The original title featured four amusing diversions, but it was in the sequel that these really came into their own. *Super Monkey Ball 2* invested a great deal of imagination in creating a joyful series of games that would bring a smile even to a vivisectionist's party. Indeed, by this point, the developers were so aware of the social potential of these they were labelled as 'party games' on the menu. Twelve games were featured, including Monkey Boat, Monkey Bowling,

Monkey Billiards, Monkey Golf, Monkey Dogfight, Monkey Soccer, Monkey Baseball and Monkey Tennis. By way of example, Monkey Fight equips two players with a monkey ball and a large boxing glove, attached by the means of a large 'comedy' spring to the ball. They are then invited to punch each other over the edge of the playing arena. Punching power-ups that fall from the sky allow the monkey pugilists to twirl their spring-loaded gloves around like medieval maces or, most amusingly, expand their size to near screen-filling proportions. It is this primary-coloured command of utter absurdity that makes *SMB* such a unique pleasure. Rarely have monkeys been funnier.

Developer: Amusement Vision; **Publisher**: Sega; **Platform**: Coin-Op, Nintendo GameCube.

Tekken
1994 (Coin-Op); 1995 (PlayStation)
Namco

Tekken is not a subtle game. This is by no means a criticism, as there is little evidence that Namco, the creators of the 'King of Iron Fist Tournament', were seeking to create a delicate or understated experience. A 3D beat-em-up, *Tekken* was clearly influenced by the aesthetic and design of Sega's *Virtua Fighter*, which had revolutionised arcades in 1993 and rejuvenated the combat game. Originally developed as an arcade game and released in 1994, *Tekken* was converted to the PlayStation the following year and, despite being among the early roster of titles for Sony's first videogames console, it has gone on to become one of the platform's most enduring franchises. To date, Namco have produced five sequels and new versions of the game are in development for PSP and PlayStation 3. Its arcade heritage notwithstanding, the history of *Tekken* is inextricably linked with that of the PlayStation. Not only did the early appearance of the game do much to promote the technical prowess of the new console, but also it allowed Namco to steal a march on its competition. While Sega struggled to convert *Virtua Fighter* for its ill-fated, PlayStation-rivalling 'Saturn' console, *Tekken* brought the pleasure and spectacle of 3D fighting into the home with flair and panache. As such, while it is obvious to note that the PlayStation brand benefited from the presence of a well-crafted and executed game like *Tekken*, it is important to recognise also that the console itself was extremely important to *Tekken*, not merely because it catapulted the game into the spotlight as it bathed in the reflected glory of Sony's all-conquering machine, but also because it was PlayStation's processing and graphics capabilities that enabled games like this to exist in the home.

Comparisons between *Tekken* and *Virtua Fighter* are inevitable and, like any 3D beat-em-up, *Tekken* owes a considerable debt to Sega's genre-defining game. However, while there may be generic similarities, such as the unremitting focus on one-on-one combat,[69] there are a number of important differences between the games and, as both titles have been treated to the home conversions they deserve, they have developed distinct characteristics and flavours. Where *Virtua Fighter* is orientated around an almost inscrutable restraint that eschews visual excess for disciplined combat, *Tekken* is an altogether more opulent affair. From the mini-explosions and puffs of smoke that accompany each successful strike; through the ability to 'juggle' characters, continually pummelling them in mid-air without allowing their limp bodies to hit the ground; the preposterous backstories told in lavish cutscenes; to the fighting kangaroos, bears and pandas that have become staples of the series, *Tekken* is an exercise in videogame fighting rather than a hand-to-hand combat simulation. However, *Tekken* is not simply dissimilar to *Virtua Fighter* in aesthetic, and has some unique takes on the beat-em-up genre as a whole. Chief among these is the interface. Since Capcom's *Street Fighter II*, control systems have used a joystick for character movement and have mapped as many as six buttons to punches and kicks of differing strengths. *Tekken*'s approach, however, is refreshingly simple. In dedicating four buttons to the four limbs of the combatants, Namco's designers crafted an intuitive system that links the player to the on screen character in a more visceral, bodily way than systems based around types of action or activity.

69. *Tekken Tag Tournament* (2000) is a notable exception to the formula that sees teams of two players duking it out.

Developer: Namco; **Publisher**: Namco; **Platform**: Coin-Op, Sony PlayStation.

Theme Park
1994
Bullfrog

With Will Wright's *Maxis* already having monopolised the market for
'*Sim*' games, one could have been forgiven for thinking there was little
point in offering 'me-too' simulation games in 1994. Peter Molyneux's
Bullfrog had already achieved huge success with their first title, *Populous*,
a game credited with inventing the 'god-game' genre. Worked on by the
young prodigy Demis Hasassbis, *Theme Park* was to make strides in
translating a sophisticated simulation model into a mass-market product.

Whereas *Championship Manager* had the established statistical
culture (and the loyalty it engenders) of football to base itself around,
Bullfrog faced a far more difficult task with making a business simulation
accessible, yet it does so with aplomb. *Theme Park* effectively wraps its
internal engine of complex business transaction within a primary-
coloured world, investing the fiscal world with a rich and fun sense of
character. Indeed, *Theme Park* was such a colourful celebration of
experience design and modern capitalism that the direct and highly
conspicuous sponsorship of the Midland Bank on some versions of it
seemed barely incongruous. Hold that thought; a videogame, sponsored
by a bank.

Like many of Molyneux's signature titles, they begin with an almost
childishly simplistic and fantastical promise; be a god! (*Populous*), run a
film studio! (*The Movies*), be a god again! (*Black and White*) and, in this
case, run your own theme park! While the surface and primary appeal of
these titles holds a pure proposition, the systems at work powering the
game are inevitably incredibly complex. And yet they *feel* simple. *Theme
Park* gives us a crowd full of apparently autonomous pixel-people, all
exercising their own free will in choosing what rides to enjoy, what fast
food to eat and where to throw up. While obviously limited in visual
complexity, these visitors are all afforded a true sense of their own
identity through an artificial intelligence system that drove them to try

and satisfy a series of basic needs and wants. One is very quickly seduced into subscribing to these visitors as real concerns and investing heavily in attempting to deliver them a great time.

Theme Park was followed by a sequel, the tenuously named *Theme Hospital*, which employed the similar management conceit and visual style, but placed it within a healthcare environment. While not as commercially successful as its predecessor, the game continued to mine the irreverent style of humour to great effect. Cannily observing that disease is rarely amusing to mainstream audiences, Bullfrog limited the ailments to fictional problems such as 'bloaty head' and 'slack tongue'. The *Theme* franchise concluded with this title, thereby avoiding a repetition of the '*Sim*' prefix series.

Publisher: Electronic Arts; **Platform**: 3DO, Commodore Amiga/Amiga CD32, MS-DOS, Sega MegaDrive, Atari Jaguar, Macintosh, Sony PlayStation, Sega Saturn, Super Nintendo Entertainment System.

Tomb Raider
1996
Core Design

So much has been written about *Tomb Raider* since its original release that it seems pointless to restate. While rightly credited with making a huge contribution to elevating videogames into the pop-media consciousness, any cursory scan of discussions about the game tends to reveal one recurring feature: the discussion is rarely about the game. The sheer iconographic weight of its heroine has obfuscated much of *Tomb Raider* itself into a secondary role to Lara Croft. One could be forgiven for thinking that the levels and mechanics of *Tomb Raider* exist only as a supporting context to its protagonist. Editorial and critical debate outside of the specialist gaming press has prevaricated endlessly on the gender stereotyping of Lara, her possible role as a post-feminist icon or possible role as constructed object for male manipulation. Certainly Lara *herself* has the autonomy to undertake product licensing deals, magazine covers and other media opportunities without the trappings of the game. Importantly, it is also difficult to ascertain which (of the many) *Tomb Raider* titles one is actually addressing in any discussion. The series descended to a low point with *Tomb Raider: Angel of Darkness* in 2003, when the critical mauling it deserved and received ended in the game's development being moved to a different studio by embattled publisher Eidos. For now, we are talking about *Tomb Raider* – the original.

So what of the actual *game*? *Tomb Raider* attempts, on many occasions successfully, to create the feeling of inhabiting a wholly open world. The player is free to explore what feel at the time like boundless environments. Its other central design concern is in the fusion of a series of establishing genres; the shoot-em-up, the puzzle game and, finally, the platform game. It is in these aspirations that *Tomb Raider* is at its most interesting and most flawed. In the earlier titles, Lara was never handled particularly well. Despite being placed in a wholly 3D world and being given puzzles and combat tasks that demand a skilful negotiation of space, Lara was never equipped with sufficient means to manoeuvre. For a body possessed of such apparent grace, the game forced the player into attempting the kinds of pixel-perfect leaps that would not have seemed out of place in *Manic Miner*.

Tomb Raider functions best as a point of transition for videogames. Most obviously pioneering their march into mainstream cultural coverage, it also served as a rehearsal for the transition of exploration, combat and puzzles into a 3D environment that would ultimately be executed far better by other titles. Without the particular character design of its USP it would never had made the same impact on pop culture, even though it would have played the same mechanic. *Tomb Raider* works helpfully as a standing conference on the importance, or not, of the presence of character within game design. What would it be without her?

As a final contemporary postscript, it was the *Tomb Raider* design (as distinct from Lara herself) that was one of two videogames nominated in the recent Design Museum/BBC TV Great British Design quest awards. Coming in at number eight in a public vote, it fell one ahead of *GTA* and one behind cat's eyes. Incidentally, Concorde won.

Publisher: Eidos; **Platform**: Sega Saturn, PC, Macintosh, Sony PlayStation.

Track and Field
1983
Konami

In recent years there has been a great deal of publicity surrounding titles such as *EyeToy Kinetic* and *Dance Dance Revolution*. Suddenly, games had arrived that not only reinvented what we thought about interfaces, but also challenged the popular perception of videogaming as a sedentary pastime. It's easy to forget that some years ago *Track and Field* was already exercising gamers into at least a moderate sweat. Directly tackling the challenge of reducing explicitly physical activity into an already existing gaming interface, Konami effectively laid the blueprint for a series of controller-busting games of the early 1980s.

The game distils six athletic events down into three buttons; two to 'run' (or swing) and one for 'action'. The running mechanic is created by the rapid pressing of each run button alternately. The faster one is able to do this, obviously, the faster one runs. It is a simple, elegant mapping of the on screen activity onto the hardware interface and this simple mashing of the arcade controls directly links the player to the physical experience of the sport they are simulating with surprising effect and the game becomes a strangely compelling challenge, particularly when multiple players are involved. Without doubt, playing *Track and Field* is an exhausting experience, perhaps not as physically demanding as the actual events being simulated, but hard work, nonetheless. There is some degree of skill here as well. Aside from the button-bashing, events such as the javelin and hammer-throw require precision timing to ensure that while the run-up delivers as much speed as possible, it does not overstep the mark and that the projectile is released at the optimum angle so as to ensure the maximum distance. Similarly, the 100-metre hurdles require a balance of raw power and perfect timing if the barriers are to be jumped rather than simply powered through.

Although there is some delicacy and precision lurking underneath the surface, *Track and Field* will be forever remembered for the visceral

Track and Field: many a joystick retired before the finishing line

battering that it encouraged the player to practise on the cabinet and its controls. While this control mechanism works very well on hardy arcade machine buttons with tough microswitches and durable parts designed for the abuses of careless and often frustrated players taking out their anger on the hardware (just as any bad workman would blame their tools), the genre was more problematic when transferred to the more fragile joysticks of home computers and consoles. On the Commodore 64 and Spectrum in particular, titles such as *Daley Thompson's Decathlon* and the Activision *Decathlon* required that players furiously waggle their sticks from left to right to gain speed. These physical demands proved rather too much for many joysticks, which gave up the ghost suffering career-ending injuries. Many a joystick and even keyboard has been sent into an early retirement as a result of an overindulgent *Track and Field* session.

Publisher: Konami; **Platform**: Coin-Op.

Trauma Center: Under the Knife
2005
Atlus

When the Nintendo DS (Dual Screen) launched in 2004, it was to the initial confusion of the games community. The Playstation Portable, Sony's recent entry into the handheld games market, was, on first sight, an immeasurably more stylish machine. With a bright, widescreen display and gloss black finish, it pandered directly to the aspirational consumer, providing the 'home cinema in your hand' experience. In direct contrast to this sleek multimedia powerhouse, the DS appeared more like a child's toy. Its light grey plastic casing followed none of the contours that might suggest a mature style, its clamshell design felt robust, practical and ever so slightly cheap in comparison to the PSP (even *Wired* magazine deigned to criticise its design as 'clunky'[70]). It became very apparent upon release, however, that the PSP and DS were not in fact competitors at all, but operated in very different cultural spaces.

The DS carried two key innovations. First, the dual screen display allowed for a partitioning of gameplay and information; second, the bottom display functioned as a touch screen (the DS came complete with a stylus). Previously being the domain of handheld organisers and cad-cam software, the touch screen wasn't an innovation that was immediately and obviously synonymous with 'fun'. While it was to be Nintendo's internal development teams that would first and best demonstrate the gameplay potentials offered by the new interface with notable early titles such as *WarioWare Touched!*, third-party developers would rapidly embrace the technology, producing radical and innovative titles that explored the hardware to its full capability. One of the most notable of these early titles is *Trauma Center: Under the Knife*. Radical, innovative and utterly aware of its own potential for fun, as the promotional site from developer Atlus states, 'Bet you've never played a game about surgery before!'[71]

Despite warnings on the start-up screen that players should not 'try the procedures at home', it quickly becomes apparent that, while gaming technologies are being piloted by health authorities all over the world to improve surgical skills, *Trauma Center* has no aspirations to being a sober surgical simulation. While delivering a challenging series of skill-based tasks, the game is as interested in the theatre as it is the operating.

Rigorously formal in its linear narrative structure, the player is propelled through a series of chapters and episodes that are illustrated by a lightly animated manga. The player is cast as a young doctor Derek Stiles (note the initials) who is a direct descendant of Asclepius, the Greek god of medicine. It's the year 2018 and all major diseases such as AIDS and cancer have been eradicated, the greatest threat to humans now is a mysterious condition known as G.U.I.L.T.. Thankfully, Derek is blessed with the gift of the 'healing touch', which allows him to take on the disease . . .

Trauma Center's characters are a deftly drawn amalgam of every medical TV drama you have ever seen. Together, they hysterically emote their way through a complex and surprisingly emotionally mature series of episodes, all of which climax in Derek scrubbing up and reaching for the scalpel.

Given the repetitive nature of the tasks involved, the surgery sections of *Trauma Center* are surprisingly engaging. Again, we have the skilful use of the dramatic conventions of hospital drama to thank for this. Using the stylus variously as scalpel, needle, ultrasound scanner, Derek is trained and guided through the operations by other characters. While being clearly guided in the task in hand, the player's challenge is one essentially of precision and speed. Underscored by a relentless pastiche of its TV movie soundtrack influences, it is almost impossible for the player not to become emotionally engaged in the sheer drama of it all as the clock ticks down and the patients' vitals fall. The palpable tension is sustained by a wholly narrative conceit that acts as a platform for a series of essentially simple tests of hand-eye co-ordination. In a next-gen climate characterised by impassioned hyperbole about the potential of 'interactive cinema', *Trauma Center: Under the Knife* stands as a shining and important challenge to the assumption that linear narratives are by definition less than engaging. Bolstered by the success of this first surgery simulator, a sequel was announced at 2006's E3 (Electronic Entertainment Expo). Destined for the Nintendo Wii console, the game comes with a delicious subtitle. *Trauma Center: Second Opinion* wears its wit proudly on the sleeve of its scrubs and would-be housemen can only begin to imagine what Atlus will do with the Wii's motion sensitive controller and where we might be encouraged to (virtually) stick it . . .

70. See <www.wired.com/wired/archive/13.02/play.html>.
71. <www.atlus.com/trauma_center/index.html>.

Publisher: Atlus; **Platform**: Nintendo DS.

Vib Ribbon
1999
NanaOn-Sha

Vib Ribbon is that rarest of things – a truly revolutionary videogame. It is not a genre-defining title. Indeed, while it was an early entrant to a now well-populated genre, and while its gameplay is markedly different from titles such as *Dance Dance Revolution* or *Beatmania*, it is by no means the first 'rhythm action' game. Superficially, *Vib Ribbon* does not even seem to have been emulated widely and, given its limited release and

Vib Ribbon: the everyday story of a rabbit that evolves into a winged princess

comparative lack of marketing, it is a game that many dedicated PlayStation owners have never even heard of, let alone played. And yet, the game *is* revolutionary.

Coming towards the end of the original PlayStation's lifecycle, when photo-realism had become the watchword and games such as *Gran Turismo* were pushing players' expectations towards meticulous mimicry and simulation, *Vib Ribbon*'s aesthetic was utterly shocking. No complex 3D models or spectacular reflection effects here. *Vib Ribbon* wasn't even in colour. Instead, this was a game presented in glorious monochrome with graphics that even eschewed the retro-chic and geometric precision of *Asteroids*' vectors in favour of scratchy, jerky, apparently hand-drawn lines that sit part-way between a child's drawing and an experimental Czech animation. Unusual, uncompromising and unapologetic, *Vib Ribbon* is completely committed to its visual style. The star of the show is Vibri, a 2D rabbit who has to be guided along an obstacle course. Superficially, this may sound like standard platform game fare, but 'obstacle course' perhaps fails to capture the economy of the pared-down gameworld. Vibri travels relentlessly along a 2D line – or ribbon – that is filled with obstructions that bar her path. There are only four basic obstacles and the player's sole task is to help Vibri over these by pressing the appropriate button combinations. It is, without doubt, one of the simplest game designs. What makes it so charming, complex and revolutionary, is that the obstacles along the ribbon are not predefined but rather are uniquely and automatically generated in response to the music track. What makes it so endlessly replayable is that the entire game code is loaded into the PlayStation's RAM, which means the game disk can be taken out and replaced with any audio CD. And so, long before 'personalisation' became the buzzword of the next generation of Xbox 360s and GameBoy Micros, and before Microsoft began extolling the virtues of ripping your own soundtracks to the Xbox's hard drive, *Vib Ribbon* put your music centre-stage. And this is not an inconsequential gimmick. The style, tempo and intensity of the music dramatically affect the nature of the ribbons, as the frequency and complexity of the obstacles generated by the game are inextricably linked with the sonic fingerprint of the music the player chooses.

To some extent, *Vib Ribbon* is the story of a rabbit that evolves into a winged princess or devolves, inexplicably, into a frog depending on how carefully and successfully the player guides them along the obstacle-ridden ribbon. But, ultimately, *Vib Ribbon* is a game about your CD collection. Playing your favourite album will never be the same again.

There have been two sequels to *Vib Ribbon*, though neither enjoyed the critical acclaim of the original. Both titles explored similar territory in generating gameworlds from personalisable raw materials. *Mojib-Ribbon* substituted *Vib Ribbon*'s music for text to create a series of challenges based around interacting with Japanese kanji characters, while *Vib Ripple* centred on digital images.

Publisher: Sony Computer Entertainment Europe; **Platform**: Sony PlayStation.

Virtua Fighter
1993
Sega AM2

The early to mid-1990s was a particularly exciting time for gamers. This was a bold new era of gaming, a genuine revolution, but the enthusiasm was not caused by the emergence of a raft of new genres, or the creation of new hero or mascot. Rather, the 1990s ushered in an era of greater depth in games, in the most literal sense. This was the age of 3D games. As the homes of cutting-edge gaming technologies, arcades had previously seen forays into three-dimensionality, with driving games leading the way, but for players at home, gaming was still a largely 2D affair. Moreover, even in the arcades, previous experiments with 3D had been limited to car racing and occasional aerial combat, like that seen in *Afterburner* and *Space Harrier*, and had made use of graphical techniques that teased and coaxed an approximation of a 3D world out of hardware designed to render 2D scenes and objects. However fun these games were in the playing, they had the look of children's toy theatres with rows of flat, 2D layers effectively stacked on top of each other to create the illusion of depth of field. True 3D remained the stuff of science fiction, as did the equally unlikely Total Immersion Virtual Reality with its headsets, motion sensors and empty promises. In 1992, Sega's *Virtua Racing* changed things decisively. Flat cars and scenery were replaced with polygonal models that moved at incredible speed and, most importantly, possessed genuine solidity. The freely selectable 'virtua viewpoints' showed this new-found depth in its full glory and allowed players to view the action from inside or outside the car, and even from a trailing helicopter that tracked the vehicle. What particularly impressed was the silky smooth way the viewpoints shifted.

However, the real shock of 3D would be felt a year later when Sega unveiled the next in its *Virtua* series. It is one thing seeing modelled versions of metal cars and static trackside objects, but quite another to be confronted with human characters moving and performing in the most lifelike way ever seen in a game. Capcom's artists had worked wonders with hand-drawn animation in games like *Street Fighter II* and had created worlds and characters with charm, distinctiveness and dynamism, but with *Virtua Fighter*, Sega's designers had added realism to the lexicon of gaming. Where *SFII* and its ilk presented their action from the fixed viewpoint of a third-person perspective that showed everything in profile, in *VF*, Sega expanded on its 'virtua viewpoints' and introduced a moving camera. To show off the solidity and 3D of *VF*'s world and characters, the camera zoomed around showing off the battling bodies from all angles. No static, paper-thin drawings these. *VF*'s combatants had fronts, backs and sides and they moved with a fluidity that had not been seen in videogame animation. Despite their name, these 'virtua' fighters were more real than players had ever witnessed. In fact, *VF*'s extraordinary verisimilitude is only partly a function of the moving game camera. By using the then-innovative technique called 'motion capture', Sega's developers had eschewed traditional animation techniques and had instead taken real human performances of punches, kicks, dodges and leaps, mapped them onto the skeletons of these computerised characters, wrapped them in shaded polygons, and given them to players to re-perform.

Virtua Fighter opened the floodgates for 3D beat-em-ups and was soon joined by games such as Namco's *Tekken* and *Soul Calibur*, and Tecmo's *Dead or Alive*. However, what distinguished Sega's game from Namco's offerings in particular or Capcom's increasingly anime-influenced 2D titles was its focus on technique, restraint and understatement. Where Capcom's games fill the screen with explosions as bone-crunching special moves connected, *Mortal Kombat* has spinal columns pulled out in infamous 'fatalities', and *Dead or Alive* sees characters crashing through windows, falling many storeys, only to continue fighting, *VF*'s simulation is altogether less histrionic, less virtual. *VF* yields little at first and novice players will find themselves defeated frequently and comprehensively. There is little to be gained from bashing randomly at the buttons, as *VF* demands something of the discipline of martial arts. Only through dedication and commitment comes skill and proficiency.

There have been three sequels to *VF* that have added new characters and capabilities such as sidestepping to evade attacks in *VF3*, for example, and some minor revisions that have tweaked the timings of moves and the balance between characters. All four current instalments have been converted to home consoles, while, in 2005, Sega announced that *VF5* is in development but have revealed scant details about the game.

Perhaps the most interesting point to note with regard to this innovative 3D beat-em-up, however, is that it is not really 3D at all. More precisely, while its characters and arenas are 3D and its camera roams freely in 3D space, its gameplay is resolutely 2D. The two fighters constantly face one another and, while they can move towards or away from their opponents, and even jump up, they cannot move off this plane and are not free to move about in 3D space. Even *VF3*'s sidestepping move only realigns the axis on which the players battle. And so, although *VF* appears utterly unlike *Street Fighter II* and the '2D' beat-em-ups it usurped, its 3D is actually something of an illusion. Perhaps it is not quite a wolf in sheep's clothing, but certainly not all is as it seems in this virtua world.

Publisher: Sega; **Platform**: Coin-Op.

WarioWare, Inc.: Mega Microgame$
2003
Nintendo

WarioWare, Inc. is defiantly and self-consciously unfashionable. It bucks almost every trend in contemporary game design. In fact, it is not even a game, per se. Rather, it is a collection of hundreds of 'micro-games', each of which last no longer than five seconds, where the objective is rarely clear and the contest is only partly about completing the ultimately simple tasks. The single biggest challenge is working out what you are supposed to do in the first place – no instructions, no tutorials, just trial and, more often than not, error. This is made all the harder as micro-games are thrown at the player randomly and in such rapid succession that there is no chance to zone in on, predict or prepare for the challenges. No sooner has the horrible realisation of the last micro-game's aim hit home than we are onto the next.

In an era of increasingly complex videogames with twisting narratives, rich characters, and pretensions to shedding the 'childish' tag of 'game' altogether in their continuing search to become interactive entertainment, *WarioWare, Inc.* is a celebration of gaming. In fact, far from attempting to dress up games as something far grander (as *Fahrenheit*), *WarioWare, Inc.* boils them down to their barest essentials, reducing them, with a precision that Einstein would have been proud of, to their absolute simplest, but no simpler. With its limited controls, deliberately minimal graphics, and only the most functional sound effects, *WarioWare, Inc.* could be easily dismissed as retro nostalgia that simply harks back to the days of Nintendo's Game & Watch series (see *Parachute*). Coupled with classic NES-themed mini-games, Nintendo is undoubtedly inviting the player to wallow in its inimitable heritage, but there is more. *WarioWare, Inc.* oozes an extraordinary confidence in its pared-down economy.

Ignoring the prevailing trends in game design could be a recipe for disaster of course. Yet *WarioWare, Inc.* has spawned a number of sequels, each of which has left the basic formula of sequences drawn

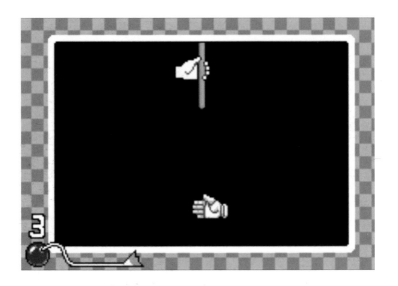

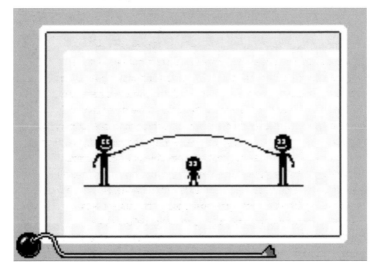

WarioWare, Inc.: accessible, innovative, audacious, silly, but above all, fun

from a smorgasbord of micro-games untouched, but has experimented with the most innovative of control methods. Where the original GameBoy Advance title employed just a few face buttons and the directional pad, its sequel (*WarioWare Twisted*) includes a gyro-sensor in the cartridge that senses the angle at which the console is held – no buttons or switches to press, literally twist the whole game console in your hands to set balls rolling down slopes or through mazes. Continuing the visceral connection, *WarioWare Touched!*, for the Nintendo DS, puts the console's touch screen to great use with different micro-games demanding different stylus skills – prodding, scrubbing, slicing, circling . . . but the coup de grâce comes with the DS's microphone. No *Nintendogs* speech recognition here though – again, things are simpler with *WarioWare*. Blow into the microphone to inflate balloons or spin windmills – both the game and the player are equally breathless. The relentless speed of the game and the physical and mental effort required to play, even just to keep up with it, makes *WarioWare* in all its guises an exhausting but hugely pleasurable experience.

Ultimately, *WarioWare, Inc.* is the poster-child for Nintendo's approach to videogames. No interactive entertainment, no hypertexts, or any other of the embarrassed (and embarrassing) euphemisms here. This is pure, unabashed gaming. Accessible, innovative, audacious, silly, but above all, fun. Genuine, laugh out loud fun. A joyous celebration of videogaming packaged in pristine five-second bursts – tailor-made for the short attention spans of the MTV generation.

Publisher: Nintendo; **Platform**: Nintendo GameBoy Advance.

WipEout
1995
Psygnosis

WipEout is a racing game set in 2105 in which players pilot 'anti-gravity' craft around a series of increasingly challenging circuits, competing for points in the WipEout leagues. The game is presented in full 3D, with the player racing 'into' the screen, and is notable for the intensity of its experience, combining highly stylised graphics, extremely fast-paced action and a soundtrack of contemporary techno music. Although a link-mode exists for simultaneous multiplayer gaming, this requires that each player has their own PlayStation, television screen and copy of the game. As such, for all but the best-equipped fans, *WipEout* is a single-player game in which the player competes against seven computer-controlled opponents. A key European launch title, *WipEout* has become synonymous with 'PlayStation chic' and the synergy of videogames, music and club cultures.

While bearing similarities to Nintendo's *F*-Zero (1990) in terms of setting and the extraordinary sense of speed, *WipEout* adds a number of elements to the mix.

Taking advantage of the PlayStation's 3D graphics capabilities, *WipEout*'s worlds are rendered with a solidity and move with a speed that few home console gamers had previously witnessed. The atmospherically lit, twisting raceways with low-roofed tunnels and high-sided barriers increase the apparent sense of speed and freneticism as corners and hairpin bends appear with little visual warning. Though they are part of the game's appeal, the sinuous tracks and limited views of the horizon were partly a response to the PlayStation's inability to draw vistas sprawling into the distance. In order to keep the pace of the game high, the tracks twist and turn in front of the player to block the horizon and limit the distance that needs to be calculated and drawn.

Weaponry such as homing missiles to hinder or even eliminate opponents and shields to provide temporary protection against enemy fire add a tactical dimension to the game. In a style similar to Nintendo's *Super Mario Kart* (released three years earlier), weapons and shields are acquired by flying over icons on the track surface which 'power up' the player's craft. The result is a game that opens the gates to a new type of gaming while simultaneously parading its gaming credentials.

As one of the most successful European launch titles for Sony's first videogame console, *WipEout* quickly became emblematic of the PlayStation brand. The game is seen as key in changing the popular perception of videogames from a pastime for nerdy boys to something of cultural significance, and recapturing the interests of gamers in their twenties who had abandoned gaming. While *WipEout* marked a graphical quantum leap for home console gamers, this was only part of the reason for its success. The inclusion of music from popular techno groups, such as The Chemical Brothers, Orbital and Leftfield, the use of The Designer's Republic to create in-game iconography and packaging materials, and the placing of playable *WipEout*/PlayStation systems in chill-out rooms in dance clubs, all gave *WipEout*, PlayStation and videogames in general a boost in cultural credibility. Through the associations with club culture, dance music and, by inference at least, drug culture that began with *WipEout* (and note also the big 'E' in the name, referencing the Ecstasy-inspired popular culture of the time) videogames not only rode the mid-1990s zeitgeist, but became embedded within it.

Developer Psygnosis was acquired by Sony in 1993 prior to the launch of PlayStation and was subsequently renamed Sony Studio Liverpool in 1999. All *WipEout* releases from this point have been PlayStation exclusives.

Publisher: Sony Computer Entertainment Europe; **Platform**: Sony PlayStation.

World of Warcraft
2004
Blizzard

Videogames and fantasy fiction have long been bedfellows, with the work of J. R. R. Tolkien and others providing a rich seam of inspiration for developers. However, the translation of the worlds, aesthetics and characters of works of fiction such as *The Hobbit* into videogames is not a simple process. In fact, the majority of fantasy fiction videogames are, to a greater or lesser extent, computerised versions of tabletop games such as *Dungeons & Dragons*. *D&D*'s structure of quests with parties of players each adopting the persona of a unique character that is drawn from a basic set of classes, races and types, and which develop is throughout play by gaining experience in battle and acquiring possessions and weapons, for example, has become the staple of videogames role-playing games (RPGs).

Certainly *World of Warcraft* (usually known to players as *WoW*) appears, superficially at least, to fit this pattern and the aesthetics of fighting and magic, the mechanics of role playing and character development, and the narrative structure of the quest are clearly derived from tabletop gaming. Two things are particularly noteworthy about *WoW*, however.

First, *WoW* is not merely an RPG like *D&D* or the various instalments of the *Warcraft* videogame series that preceded it, but rather is an 'MMORPG': a 'Massively Multiplayer Online Role Playing Game'. That is, unlike traditional multiplayer games that may support two, four or even eight simultaneous players crowded around a monitor or TV screen, each clasping a controller, *WoW* supports many tens of thousands of players simultaneously, each connected to the *WoW* world via their Internet-connected home computers. This is made possible because *WoW*'s gameworld is persistent. It does not reside on the local hard drives of players but rather on external servers that each of the many players logs into when they wish to play. As a result, the world continues to evolve and change whether individual players visit it or not. One knock-on effect of this is that players tend to spend a considerable amount of time in *WoW* for fear that something important might happen in their absence. As such, both repeat play and long play sessions are commonplace. The compellingly 'addictive' nature of the game has led to it being referred to as 'World of Warcrack' by many of its fans.[72]

Second, *WoW*'s fanbase is absolutely huge. Since the game's release in late 2004, its audience has grown to over six million active subscribers as of February 2006, according to its developer.[73] *WoW* was not the first MMORPG and even accepting the resurgence in interest in fantasy fiction triggered by Peter Jackson's *Lord of the Rings* movie adaptations, the success of a complex *D&D*-style game might come as something of a surprise. Certainly Blizzard benefited from the earlier work of other MMORPG developers, particularly with regard to game balance, dealing with players returning to the game after time away, and the imposition of a consensual system of player vs player (PvP) combat that sidesteps the issue of unsuspecting characters being attacked and killed for their hard-earned equipment and treasure.[74] Perhaps most significant, however, is the game design decision to offer 'instance dungeons' that lends *WoW* something of the feel, familiarity and structure of an offline RPG. Instance dungeons are essentially quests that are tailored for groups of particular sizes and that, importantly, are uniquely created for each group that enters. As a result, a group in an instanced dungeon cannot be interrupted by other players on the 'outside', nor can they simply summon a legion of followers to overpower the foes lurking within. Instance dungeons allow for more complex quests and typically benefit from a strong narrative structure. Perversely, then, at least one of the strengths of *WoW* as a game is its ability to overcome some of the limitations of MMORPGs through the simulation of a smaller-scale multiplayer gaming experience.

There is more to *WoW* than gaming, however. This is an eminently social environment in which talk and chatter are as much a part of the experience as swordplay and spells. Blizzard's official websites promote discussion of the game on their forums, actively encouraging the production and sharing of fan art, screenshots from the game, wallpapers and even comics among the community.[75]

72. See the 'World of Warcrack' fansite for more information. Available at <www.worldofwarcrack.com>.

73. See Blizzard press releases at <www.blizzard.com/press/060228.shtml>. Note also, that 5 million was announced just three months earlier in December 2005. See <www.blizzard.com/press/051219.shtml>.

74. See Blizzard's rules for more information in PvP combat at <www.wow-europe.com/en/info/basics/guide.html#eight>.

75. See Blizzard's 'community' pages at <www.worldofwarcraft.com/community>.

Publisher: Vivendi; **Platform**: PC, Macintosh.

Yoshi Touch & Go
2005
Nintendo

It sounds like the beginning of a bad videogaming joke: what do you call a platform game with no platforms? It is not, however, and instead of a facetious punchline, we have one of the most innovative videogames to emerge in the twenty-first century. *Yoshi Touch & Go* (originally titled *Catch! Touch! Yoshi!* in Japan) was released in 2005 for the Nintendo DS and, unlike launch titles such as *Super Mario 64 DS* that reheated an albeit peerless game and added some DS flourishes like a touch screen control system, it utterly embraces all that the DS has to offer. Accordingly, with the possible exception of *WarioWare Touched!*, it is the most effective and capable demonstration of the DS's capabilities and is the most lucid and effortless expression of these technical capacities in gameplay. Learning a little of the game's development history, this is perhaps unsurprising as the title began its life as a Nintendo technical demonstration designed not with commercial release in mind but rather to communicate to potential developers and partners the host of radical new features of the host console.[76] However, so successful was the implementation at trade shows that the demo was upgraded in status and put into full development.

Yoshi Touch & Go is centred around a similar premise to *Super Mario World 2: Yoshi's Island* and finds Baby Mario and Luigi kidnapped by the evil Kamek, only here Baby Mario is dropped en route and so the action begins with him plummeting towards the ground. The player's task is to guide the descending infant to safety by creating slides and chutes out of clouds, steering the little one away from the spiked hazards and flying enemies intent on attacking him. Upon successfully gliding through the treacherous skies, Baby Mario falls to Earth but there to break his fall is Yoshi the dinosaur who, from here on, is the star of the show. The remainder of the game is played out across a series of horizontally scrolling stages that are superficially similar to previous *Super Mario* titles.

However, there is a significant difference. Yoshi may well be the hero of the piece and the character with whom the player most clearly identifies, yet he is not under their direct control. Rather, Yoshi marches inexorably across the landscape – a landscape peppered with gaping chasms, and ground and airborne enemies.

And so, rather than manoeuvre Yoshi with the usual up, down, left, right and jump controls, here the player's task is to affect and modify the environment itself so as to provide a safe route for Yoshi and Baby Mario. This indirect control of the character is achieved in the most direct manner by drawing on the screen. Using their stylus, the player creates pathways of clouds upon which Yoshi can scramble. A platform game with no platforms? Not quite, but the player does have to create them themselves. And to eradicate cloud paths? Well, blow into the microphone and they disappear into wispy nothingness.

Given the intention to illustrate the potential of the system, it is hardly a surprise to witness the manner in which each of the DS's innovations are harnessed and showcased. What is surprising, however, is the seamless manner in which the dual screens set-up, the touch screen input and the built-in microphone are integrated into the game. Thanks to Nintendo's matchless design, they are at once shockingly new and reassuringly familiar and intuitive. The dual screens are expertly handled and high-level planning and forethought are essential if cloud platforms drawn on the lower screen are to have the desired effect once they have scrolled to the upper screen. Moreover, the way in which the action of the game is split across the two screens demands an extraordinary degree of multitasking as players are forced to split their attentions between immediate and imminent dangers coming from all angles.

Ultimately, what is interesting about *Yoshi Touch & Go* is not simply its superior design and execution, but its referentiality. Like many Nintendo titles, such as *Super Mario Kart*, it clearly foregrounds the company's gaming heritage in evoking memories of *Yoshi's Island* both in game structure, premise and aesthetics, and also signals a return to classic game design principles in returning to a structure that privileges the high score as a device for encouraging replay. More than this, however, *Yoshi Touch & Go* is a platform game about platform games and it plays with the very ideas of the genre and, indeed, the practice of game design itself. With the stylus, touch screen and microphone, the player is essentially given a platform game construction set and offered an opportunity to make their own game.

76. See <www.gamespot.com/ds/action/yoshi/review.html>.

Publisher: Nintendo; **Platform**: Nintendo DS.

References

Bennett, T. and Woollacott, J. (1987), *Bond and Beyond: The Political Career of a Popular Hero* (London: Macmillan).

Buckingham, D. and Sefton-Green, J. (2003), 'Gotta Catch 'em All: Structure, Agency and Pedagogy in Children's Media Culture', *Media, Culture & Society* vol. 25 no. 3, pp. 379–99.

Cumberbatch, G. (1998), 'Media Effects: The Continuing Controversy', in A. Briggs and P. Cobley (eds), *The Media: An Introduction* (Harlow: Longman).

Cumberbatch, G. (2004), 'Video Violence: Villain or Victim', *Video Standards Council* (*VSC*). Available at <www.videostandards.org.uk/sections/videoviolence/v1.html>.

David, C. and Shoemaker, B. (n.d.), 'The History of Sonic the Hedgehog', *Gamespot* [online]. Available at <www.gamespot.com/gamespot/features/video/hist_sonic/index.html> (accessed March 2006).

Eisenberg, R. L. (1998), 'Girl Games: Adventures in Lip Gloss', *Gamasutra* (13 February) [online]. Available at <www.gamasutra.com/features/19980213/girl_games.htm> (accessed March 2006).

Friedman, T. (2002), 'Civilization and its Discontents: Simulation, Subjectivity, and Space' [online]. Available at <www.game-research.com/art_civilization.asp>.

Griffiths, M. (2005), 'Video Games and Health: Video Gaming is Safe for Most Players and can be Useful in Health Care', *British Medical Journal* 331 (16 July), pp. 122–3. Available online at <bmj.bmjjournals.com/cgi/content/full/331/7509/122>.

Haddon, Leslie (1988), 'Electronic and Computer Games, the History of an Interactive Medium', *Screen* vol. 29 no. 2, pp. 52–75.

Jenkins, H. and Squire, K. (2003), 'Understanding Civilization (III)', *The Education Arcade* [online]. Available at <educationarcade.org/node/113>.

Kent, S. L. (2001), *The Ultimate History of Video Games: From Pong to Pokémon and Beyond – The Story Behind the Craze that Touched our Lives and Changed the World* (Roseville, CA: Prima).

Kohler, Kris (2005), *Power-up: How Japanese Video Games Gave the World an Extra Life* (Indianapolis: BradyGAMES).

Krzywinska, T. (2002), 'Hands-On Horror', in G. King and T. Krzywinska (eds), *Screenplay: Cinema/Videogames/Interfaces* (London and New York: Wallflower Press).

Leone, M. (2005), 'Thinking Outside of the Box', feature, *We ♥ Katamari*. *1-Up* [online]. Available at <1up.com/do/feature?pager.offset=0&cld=3142234>.

Newman, J. (2002), 'In Search of the Videogame Player: The Lives of Mario', *New Media and Society* vol. 4 no. 3, pp. 407–25.

Newman, J. (2004), *Videogames* (London: Routledge).

Newman, J. (2005), 'Playing (with) Videogames', *Convergence: The International Journal of Research into New Media Technologies* vol. 11 no. 1, pp. 48–67.

Newman, J. and Oram, B. (2006), *Teaching Videogames* (London: BFI Education).

Newman, J. and Simons, I. (eds) (2004), *Difficult Questions About Videogames* (Nottingham: Suppose Partners).

Poole, S. (2000), *Trigger Happy: The Inner Life of Videogames* (London: Fourth Estate).

Rollings, A. and Morris, D. (2000), *Game Architecture and Design* (Scottsdale, AZ: Coriolis).

Salen, K. and Zimmerman, E. (2003), *Rules of Play: Game Design Fundamentals* (Cambridge, MA, and London: MIT).

Sheff, D. (1993), *Game Over: Nintendo's Battle to Dominate an Industry* (London: Hodder and Stoughton).

Sherman, B. (2006), 'Story Mechanics as Game Mechanics in Shadow of the Colossus', *Gamasutra* [online]. Available at: <gamasutra.com/features/20060328/sherman_01.shtml> (accessed 3 April 2006).

Spufford, F. (2003), *Backroom Boys: The Secret Return of the British Boffin* (London: Faber and Faber).

Index

Page numbers in *italics* denote illustrations; those in **bold** indicate detailed analysis; *n* = endnote

List of Illustrations

Whilst considerable effort has been made to correctly identify the copyright holders, this has not been possible in all cases. We apologise for any apparent negligence and any omissions or corrections brought to our attention will be remedied in any future editions.

1942, Capcom; *Advance Wars*, Nintendo; *Asteroids*, Atari; *Cannon Fodder*, Virgin Interactive; *Championship Manager*, Domark; *Deus Ex*, Eidos Interactive; *Donkey Kong*, Nintendo; *Dr Kawashima's Brain Training*, Nintendo; *Ecco the Dolphin*, Sega; *EyeToy: Play*, Sony Computer Entertainment Europe; *God of War*, Sony Computer Entertainment; *Harvest Moon*, Natsume; *Killer 7*, Capcom; *The Legend of Zelda: Ocarina of Time*, Nintendo; *Manhunt*, Rockstar Games; *Metroid*, Nintendo; *Mr Do!*, Universal; *Pac-Man*, Midway; *Pokémon (Blue and Red)*, Nintendo; *Pong*, Atari; *Porrasturvat (Stair Dismount)*, tAAt; *Puzzle Bobble*, Taito; *Shadow of the Colossus*, Sony Computer Entertainment Europe; *SingStar*, Sony Computer Entertainment; *Sonic the Hedgehog*, Sega; *Space Invaders*, Midway; *Spheres of Chaos*, n/a; *Street Fighter II*, Capcom; *Super Mario 64*, Nintendo; *Super Mario Bros.*, Nintendo; *Super Mario Kart*, Nintendo; *Track and Field*, Konami; *Vib Ribbon*, Sony Computer Entertainment Europe; *WarioWare, Inc.: Mega Microgame$*, Nintendo.